In this short & very readable b·
and how employers should care fo.
I hope it will also inspire more Carer associations around
the world to create equivalents of Employers for Carers,
which has had such an influence on policy for carers in
the UK.

*— Baroness Jill Pitkeathley,*
*Co-chair All-Party Parliamentary Group on Caring*

{Take Care} should become required reading for those
wishing to understand, introduce and develop great policies and practice for working carers.

*— Ian Peters, Chairman Employers for Carers, UK*

David has been pushing forward the agenda on responsible business for many years. He is very much doing so
again now with Take Care, challenging us to think about
how employers can help their working care-givers - and
crucially why it makes good business sense to do so.

*— Momo Mahadav\President & CEO,*
*Maala\Business for Social Responsibility, Israel*

We live in an ageing society, so it is critical that people
are able to work for as long as they need and want to.
Helping workers with caring commitments makes it possible for more of them to stay in work or return to work.
David Grayson has produced a compelling case with
plenty of practical and successful examples from around
the world.

*— Andy Briggs, Chief executive officer of Aviva*
*UK Life and Chairman of Global Life &*
*Government Business Champion for Older Workers*

# ABOUT THE BOOK

*Employers large and small need to take care*!
They are at risk of losing some of their most valued and valuable employees. They will not lose these employees to competitors or to self-employment but to the employees' loved ones for whom the employees have significant caring responsibilities. The average UK workforce today will have at least one in every nine employees who are juggling their job with caring for a loved one. In Canada, this is 1:3. This may be a parent or elderly relative; a partner; a disabled son or daughter or a close friend.

Caring is a natural part of life — it is fundamental to the human condition. Many of us, when we start caring for someone, don't think of ourselves as a 'carer'. We are simply doing what comes naturally as a loving son or daughter, partner, parent. Sometimes, caring can be a short episodic burst — perhaps when a loved one needs help to recover after an operation or is suffering from severe depression. Other voluntary carers may be caring long-term and the amount of their caring progressively increases. Many working carers simply give up on juggling work, caring and personal life and quit their jobs. This can be bad for them (the negative caring nexus: greater financial pressures, greater social isolation, poor physical and mental health); bad for their employers (loss of institutional memory, productivity and of experienced and talented staff); and bad for society as employees with caring responsibilities who feel forced to quit their jobs, will have lower pensions and fewer savings to fall back on in later life and will, therefore, be more dependent on the state.

Yet it need not be like this. Smart (as well as responsible) employers understand the business as well as the moral case for helping employees with caring responsibilities to stay in work. Such organisations identify their employee carers, offer flexible and home-working, carer-leave, support internal networks of employee carers, provide access to advice and information, and continuously learn and improve, through exchanges with other employers as well as regular feedback from employees.

# TAKE CARE

## How to be a Great Employer for Working Carers

BY

### David Grayson

United Kingdom – North America – Japan
India – Malaysia – China

Emerald Publishing Limited
Howard House, Wagon Lane, Bingley BD16 1WA, UK

First edition 2017

**British Library Cataloguing in Publication Data**
A catalogue record for this book is available from the British Library

ISBN: 978-1-78714-293-0 (Print)
ISBN: 978-1-78714-292-3 (Online)
ISBN: 978-1-78714-917-5 (Epub)

ISOQAR certified
Management System,
awarded to Emerald
for adherence to
Environmental
standard
ISO 14001:2004.

**ISOQAR**
REGISTERED

Certificate Number 1985
ISO 14001

FSC
www.fsc.org
MIX
Paper from
responsible sources
FSC® C013604

INVESTOR IN PEOPLE

Dedicated to the memory of Patricia Grayson
(1922–2015).

# CONTENTS

## PART 2

## SEVEN STEPS TO BEING A GOOD EMPLOYER FOR WORKING CARERS

# PART 3

# BUILDING A MOVEMENT

# LIST OF DIAGRAMS

**PART 3, Chapter 3**

# LIST OF PHOTOGRAPHS

*There are only four kinds of people in the world — those who have been caregivers, those who are currently caregivers, those who will be caregivers and those who will need caregivers.*

*— Rosalynn Carter, Former First Lady of the USA and founder of The Rosalynn Carter Institute for Caregiving*

# FOREWORD BY ARA CRESSWELL

While there are a plethora of resources available internationally to describe the role of family and friend carers, the pressures upon them, their contribution to both the people they care for and to the wider society and what supports they need to sustain them, not all are written in the absorbing, down-to-earth and reader-friendly way that David has mastered.

While David has canvassed a range of issues relating to the caring role, the focus on combining work and care has particular resonance for an Australian audience.

Several times throughout this publication Australia's good record in recognising both the value and needs of carers is cited. It is indeed true that carers have achieved a high profile accompanied by a more supportive policy environment in the last decade.

The national government and many states have introduced Carers Recognition Acts which formally recognise and value the role of carers, acknowledge that they have their own legitimate needs for support within and beyond their caring role, recognise that they should be regarded as partners in care by medical professions and other service providers which support those they provide care to, and embody charters for carers and place obligations on public service agencies to honour those charters. (Unfortunately the penalties for not observing the admonitions of the Acts are negligible.)

In 2014 changes were made to the national Fair Work Act 2009 (which sets national employment standards) to recognise an entitlement for unpaid carers of up to 10 days of paid personal/carer's leave which can be accumulated from year to year.

Very importantly, the social security system incorporates a Carer Payment for carers who cannot work because of the demands upon them as carers and who meet a means test. It is roughly the equivalent of the Age Pension and is indexed to average male weekly earnings. In addition, a fortnightly indexed Carer Allowance of AU $124.75 is available to assist with the additional costs of caring for carers providing substantial care. Carers on the Carer Payment, Carer Allowance and Veteran's pensions are also eligible for a lump-sum annual payment of AU $600. The Carer Allowance and the annual payment are available to carers even if they study or work.

Both the national and state and territory governments also contribute to the costs of providing carer support services. In particular, the focus on carers being able to combine work and care has assumed a very high profile in recent years. The reasons are varied, but for government a particularly compelling reason arises from a preoccupation with the long-term economic cost of social security. The research shows clearly that the longer people stay out of employment because of their caring responsibilities, the less likely they will be able to return to employment when their caring role diminishes or ends. They will very likely simply transition to another, albeit less generous, social welfare payment and, in the absence of their capacity to accumulate superannuation benefits, will be reliant on the aged pension when they are past working age.

Persuading employers of the value of recruiting or keeping carers in their employ is a more challenging task. David's book canvasses in detail the case for employers from the perspective of their business interests — including the benefits of keeping experienced employees, reducing the costs of recruitment, the value of a loyal workforce and the benefits of workforce diversity which has become a prominent theme in management and business literature.

Importantly, David highlights that a carer-friendly workplace is not just a matter of employers taking on carers or keeping them on where they acquire caring responsibilities or the caring role intensifies. As a number of carer stories in this book highlight, the understanding and support of managers and co-workers is particularly important. This means that a truly carer friendly workplace makes the effort to educate all its employers about the role of carers, not just the human resources parts of the enterprise.

A workplace which values carers and wishes to assist them to combine work and care will also make information available about where carers can get support and services outside the workplace.

David has identified a range of strategies, models and case studies for creating carer friendly workplaces which will be of great assistance in the campaign to capture the hearts, minds and hip pocket nerve of employers and foster a commitment to assist their employees to combine work and care.

Ara Cresswell
*CEO Carers Australia*

# FOREWORD BY IAN PETERS

'No one should need to care alone'. This rallying cry from Carers UK's 50th anniversary campaign should equally apply to those who juggle work and caring responsibilities. However, employers' attitudes towards working carers generally significantly lag that for parents with children.

I have known David Grayson for over 20 years in various capacities, most recently as colleagues on the board of Carers UK. It is entirely consistent with David's long held conviction that employers can be forces for good, that his personal experiences of caring so articulated in this book, have led him to what should become required reading for those wishing to understand, introduce and develop great policies and practice for working carers.

In his own words, this book is a cross between a 'how to guide and a call to action'. David lays out a seven step approach from discovering the need through to monitoring the effectiveness of policies. I confess that as the former leader of a large organisation quoted by David as an exemplar in this field, we felt our way there by listening and acting. This blueprint would have been really helpful 10 years ago!

David brilliantly combines the power of individual stories with a deep insight into worldwide analysis of what has worked, what has failed, the challenges and opportunities. From Helen at Westpac in the preface, to his own story, to Craig Hughes and James Melville-Ross as exemplar leaders, the stories drive home his insights in a compelling and memorable way.

Demographics in the developed world make it clear why this book should be read by multiple audiences from business leaders, to HR professionals, academics to policy makers. Caring is becoming a universal human experience. In the United Kingdom 1 in 9 employees are carers, with that rising to 1 in 6 for those aged 45–64. By 2030 that will be 1 in 6 and 1 in 3 — a figure already reached in Canada. Once an employee spends 5 hours per week caring, it impacts their work, health and often earnings potential. Without the necessary empathy, information, flexibility and support far too many leave the workplace.

Retaining that experience, returning former carers to the workplace, and recruiting young carers makes good business sense. It is not corporate philanthropy.

There is no single template on what will work for every organisation, but the book highlights three common pillars: leadership by example; supportive and empowered line management; flexibility to changing individual circumstances.

David lays out many examples of great practice, which are often set in a wider context of a commitment to diversity, inclusivity and corporate responsibility. He highlights the opportunities created by existing and emerging technologies to redefine both support for working carers and also new forms of self-employment and collaborative enterprise for those combining work and care.

He shows how non-UK countries now lead the way in carers leave, with France and Belgium using fiscal incentives to grow local support businesses.

The book is uplifting but also sobering. While much has been done by many enlightened companies and governments, much remains to be done. Adoption is hugely variable; SMEs are largely not yet engaged; employers cannot fully address the issue without high quality local care provision and supportive public policy; too many organisations have 'hidden carers' concerned about the perceived adverse impacts of declaring they are carers.

David admits to being an optimist and a campaigner. Encouragingly he has a track record of success. This book will increase the probability of success in this area.

In my capacity as Chair of Employers for Carers (EfC) in the United Kingdom, the only self-financing employer led carers group in the world, I share David's aims and optimism. EfC has built a membership base representing over 1.25 million employees and an easily accessible compendium of best policy and practice. We have doubled our membership in 3 years as awareness grows, and we now sit at the table of government policy.

The provision of excellent workplace support for carers is a fourfold win: for the carer; for the employer; for the wider economy through higher tax and lower benefits; and importantly for the person being cared for.

David's book should help accelerate the momentum and I commend him for his initiative and passion.

Ian Peters

*Chairman Employers For Carers*

# PREFACE

*Work: the chance to be me!*

"It's not just a question of the money. It's the opportunity to use my experience and skills, to contribute to my workplace and community, and to enjoy some social life among a wonderful group of supportive colleagues. Very importantly, it gives me the chance to be just me, "Helen" the person, as well as the loving mother and carer of Ben."

Together with her husband Peter, Helen Johnson has cared for her profoundly disabled 24-year-old son Ben since his birth. Ben was diagnosed with Rubinstein-Taybi Syndrome (RTS) at birth and has a severe intellectual disability, medical, physical and sensory complications due to a further diagnosis of Autism Spectrum Disorder at 3 years of age.

Sadly, Ben also became a paraplegic in 2009 after an 'unexplained' postoperative complication causing an 'incomplete spinal cord injury'. To date Ben has had to endure 54 surgical procedures all in Melbourne, 180 km from the family home in the Australian state of Victoria.

The Johnson family has faced intense financial and emotional distress. In addition to Ben needing 24-hour care, his disabilities have come with enormous medical, specialised equipment and other associated costs. Helen says caring is a 'tough job'.

'It is financially restraining, emotionally stressful and complex... so much goes into organising your own life and someone else's as well'.

When Helen gave birth to Ben, her employer — the Australian bank Westpac Banking Corporation — gave her as much 'Carers Leave' as required.

However, when Ben was 3 years of age, 'I could not envisage my ability to return to work due to his chronic illness and the 24/7 care needs I was required to provide therefore, I sadly resigned from Westpac in 1996'.

In 2003 an ex bank manager opened her own Financial Broker Service and asked Helen to join her on a casual basis, even though Helen continued to need a great deal of time off due to Ben's medical needs and health challenges.

'However, after 12 months a particular Westpac Manager heard I had returned to work and approached me to return to Westpac on a casual or part-time basis. Of course I jumped at the chance, and returned as a casual employee with the agreement of 100% work flexibility, as Ben was, and continues to be, my number one priority. I continue to be employed with Westpac to this day but I have now obtained a permanent part-time position with an on-going agreement and permission to have work flexibility to support Ben whenever required'.

Helen has received the full support of her workplace managers and colleagues at Traralgon and now Morwell Westpac branches in Victoria, which has enabled her to work part-time while still attending to Ben's immediate needs, countless visits to specialists and frequent surgeries

'My wonderful Managers and work colleagues continually provide me with amazing flexibility and understanding with my arrival times in the morning as often I don't know what to expect each morning when entering Ben's room to help prepare and get him ready for the day.

Firstly, you would not believe the enormously long medical regime we have to go through for Ben, however when the 'odd' surprise is thrown in with the "everyday" stuff that's when it is NOT a GOOD START TO THE DAY!

Some mornings (or in the late hours of the night or early hours of the morning) I would enter his room and it would be like a murder scene because he has put his fingers so far up his nose (he loves holes) that he would have a continual blood nose and he would smear blood everywhere!

However, it is a really bad morning (or night) when I enter his room and I discover he has managed to dislodge his continence pad and managed to smear faeces over every part of his body, in his mouth, in his ears, up his nose, in his hair and all over his bed. This is why I am required to do 2 to 3 hourly night checks on him every night and we also have to ensure his catheter is flowing and not blocked and that he is comfortable due to his minimal ability to move and re-position his body.

It is also not unusual for him to have a small vomit in the night and of course because he cannot call out to us, he just has his little "silent vomit" makes sure he can smear a majority of it over every part of bed and himself and then quietly lays his head straight back down and continues to snore! He truly is a placid young man'.

## THE IMPORTANCE OF WORK IN THE CARING JOURNEY

As Helen says: 'It's not just a question of the money. It's the opportunity to use my experience and skills, to contribute to my workplace and community, and to enjoy some social life among a wonderful group of supportive colleagues. Very importantly, it gives me the chance to be just me, "Helen" the person, as well as the loving mother and carer of Ben'.

'Although my job in the bank is demanding I continually say, I go to work for my sanity and for my "respite". My work life helps me keep sane! I know I would not be the person I am today, without my employment. I also believe without my work, my own emotional mental

health and well-being would be challenged. It gives me
the necessary social opportunities and connections.
Working gives me a meaningful purpose, separate from
my intense caring role. It gives me my own independence,
enables me to contribute financially towards my family's
needs and helps create financial sustainability for our
future'.

What did it feel like when Helen gave up work to care
full-time for Ben?

'I felt emotionally devastated, ripped off and extremely
sad. I felt we were financially crippled because we had
just built a house based on having two salaries. I felt very
low, as if life had been pulled out from under me.
Everything I had worked so hard for, I felt I had lost all
my dreams. I had so many fears. What use will I be to my
family, to both my sons but especially my son with severe
and multiple disabilities? How will I manage to care for
him when I know nothing?'

Helen is very honest about the mental health issues she
encountered and how much she benefitted from a counsellor whose own son had been severely injured in a
driveway accident from a car. 'She showed me that my
feelings were ok and normal and that I can and will get
through this'.

## HOW EMPLOYER SUPPORT MAKES A DIFFERENCE

'I am so proud to have Westpac as my employer as it
truly is supportive to its employees and especially to those
who are carers. Another example is when an employee is
applying for Annual Leave; on the electronic leave request

it has a question, 'Are you applying for annual leave to care for someone or for medical reasons?' Also some of the Westpac Employee Perspective Surveys asks the Question: Are you a Carer? Do you Care for somebody? I think these questions are an example of a sincere, carer-focussed company who truly cares about its employees and their overall health and wellbeing. My managers, work colleagues & Westpac (as an employer) have been SO supportive to me as an unpaid family carer and to my family situation with regular reminders that 'family comes first' and 'family life work balance'. I am forever grateful for their amazing on-going support'.

Twenty plus years on and you don't need to speak to Helen for very long, before realising she is a great example of the old adage that 'if you want something doing, ask a busy person!' Besides caring for Ben and working for Westpac, Helen also works two days a week at a State-wide Disability Support Service in Melbourne as a Parent Support Worker and an NDIS Education Facilitator. This workplace is 360 km round trip from home requiring an early start and would not be possible without the support of her husband (Ben's father) Peter, as he also engages in flexible Carer work hours to enable Helen to leave early in the mornings.

Helen is also a National Carer Ambassador for Carers Australia and in 2015 received a Nomination for 'Australian of the Year' and although she did not win she said it was an absolute honour to have received this National recognition for her passion and dedication in advocating for and on behalf of Carers across Australia. She also sits on a number of federal government consultative committees for carers and disability, which meet in

Canberra. Helen is also a Volunteer Board Member for a local Gippsland Disability Service Provider — Interchange Gippsland and a Volunteer Board Director for Carers Victoria which is a State-wide Carer Service. She has served on both Boards for over 10 years and she is currently the Vice President of both organisations. Also, Helen recently received a Life Membership to Carers Victoria for her passion and ongoing commitment to creating positive change for Carers throughout Victoria and Australia.

Her advice to other carers? 'Never say never! I thought it would be impossible to return to work after Ben was born. Be honest with your employer: I know some people choose not to talk about home life and their personal caring situation – especially men – but if possible, it is important to do so, because employers can't assist and support you if they don't know of your caring responsibilities. Many more employers are attempting to support their employees who are family Carers but it has to be a two-way street and I believe good communication with your Manager's and Work Colleagues is the key. If possible, whilst on Carers Leave, keep connected with your employer: sometimes it is hard to think beyond your caring role but it is important to ensure a smooth transition back to work when it is possible to do so!'

Despite being an intensive, long-term carer, Helen can also work because she has an employer that strives to be a great employer for working carers, she has supportive line-managers, understanding co-workers, customers who want to be served by Helen because of her empathy and vitality, employer policies for flexible working, carer leave, a relevant EAP (Employee Assistance Programme)

# INTRODUCTION

## WORKING AND CARING: THIS IS PERSONAL

**Photo courtesy of Michael Holt.**

This book is dedicated to my mother Patricia Grayson (1922–2015).

She is the reason why I have written this book.

Mum was a primary-school teacher for almost 40 years. She graduated with distinction from Edgehill Teaching College in 1942. Apart from one term teaching in York, all the schools she taught at were in Sheffield and subsequently in North East Derbyshire. Her early classes in the Darnall and Attercliffe areas of Sheffield in the later years of World War II and immediately

afterwards had more than 60 pupils. On a very conserva-
tive estimate, given the much larger class sizes she faced
in the early years of her career, there were more than
1500 people whose early years of schooling were at the
hands of mum.

A couple of days before mum died, Louise — the student nurse who accompanied the district nurse for much
of mum's final, palliative care at home — arrived with
some additional medication. She had collected it from a
local pharmacy and was keen to report the exchange she
had just had with the lady handing over the medication:

'It is for Mrs Grayson? She taught me. She was the
best teacher I ever had!'

As mum's neighbour Pauline also discovered over the
years, that was not an unusual experience. In doctors'
waiting rooms, at bus-stops, in shops and restaurants,
there would be a familiar routine. Someone would look
over, nervously smile and finally approach mum with a
similar message of gratitude and appreciation.

As Dame Julia Cleverdon wrote after mum's death:

'Your mother influenced generations to step up to their
responsibilities — to give more and get more from their
lives.'

Mum's gift for engaging young children never left her.
Penny Hawley described bringing her two young sons
Hew and Eddy on several Christmas visits to South Ridge
towards the end of mum's life:

'As you might have gathered from my questions at the
time, I was worried about bringing the boys along to
meet her, because most of us age more in our ideas and
attitudes than our bodies and struggle to remember why
small children are curious and inconvenient. Not the

marvellous Mrs Grayson who welcomed us all and clearly delighted in chatting with Hew about iPads and the other things he was interested in. She had such warmth and enthusiasm that she captivated us all. The inspiration she must have been to the hundreds of children who passed through her classroom shone through'.

Shortly before her 90th birthday, I encouraged mum to write down a list of some of her happiest moments. As might be anticipated, many of the moments involved the family but several of the happiest memories that she had listed first were about things in her teaching career. I believe mum was a great teacher because she genuinely cared for and was always interested in people. As her great-nephew Sam wrote on her 90th birthday poster: 'she lit up the room' and as he wrote on hearing of her death: 'she made you feel so loved whenever she saw you'.

In similar vein, her great-niece Caroline wrote: 'she always remembered every detail of what I was up to! She was a fantastic lady … and like a fifth grandparent'.

Mum and I always enjoyed a close and loving relationship, as only children in particular usually do with their parents. On my 11th birthday, she and my late father had to rush me into Sheffield Children's Hospital. What the local GP had days earlier diagnosed as a sprained knee was actually a rare and life-threatening bone disease in the hip: osteomyelitis, complicated by septicaemia. I was critically ill. For several days, it was touch and go whether I would live or die. Subsequently, the specialists suggested that if I lived, my parents might have to face the prospect that I would not walk again. Happily, the medics exaggerated. It was, however, to be a year before

I did walk again — on crutches and several years before I could walk unaided. Meantime, I had my left hip removed and I spent many months in a hip-spiker (a plaster of Paris casing from my upper chest to my toes — with strategically placed holes) whilst my leg, minus hip, fused in the hip-socket. Throughout this time, my mum never missed a day's hospital visiting. Whenever it was possible, mum nursed me at home, giving up her teaching job to do so. At the age when children are learning to grow more independent of their parents, I became entirely dependent again on mine — and especially my mother — to take care of my bodily functions, feed me, keep me distracted, reassure me. Mum didn't just care for me physically. She also helped me to deal with the 'why is this happening to me? If there is a God, why is He doing this to me?' despair and anger. Mum subsequently returned to teaching, in substantial part to pay for me to go to a good school and then to Cambridge — the first person in my family to go to university. Mum subsequently took early retirement from teaching to care for her mother at home. In time, she also cared for her best friend and then became carer for my father in his final years.

## Becoming Mum's Carer

So, decades after mum nursed me through the osteomyelitis, when first dad and then my mum started to need more help, it just seemed the natural thing to try and do my very imperfect best to help them and support them. Caring for loved ones after all is part of the human condition, part of what it is to be fully human, part of the natural rhythm of life, as the quotation from Rosalynn Carter reminds us. I certainly didn't think of myself as a 'carer' — just a son helping his parents and looking after them. In all likelihood, I would have continued as a 'hidden' or non-self-identifying carer, but for Helena Herklots. Helena and I had previously served together for 5 years, on the board of a major social enterprise providing sheltered housing and domiciliary paid care for older people. Helena had often heard me at board meetings, ask whether I would accept something being proposed for clients, if it was for my own parents, in evaluating proposals. Shortly after she became CEO of the charity *Carers UK*, Helena got in touch again and invited me for a coffee. When we met, she quietly explained that at any one time in the United Kingdom, 6.5 million Britons are caring unpaid for a loved one — and that Carers UK is there to help and support these carers. Then she dropped the bait! 'Many people don't think of themselves or identify as a carer'. She paused. I smiled. I took the bait! Three months later I joined the board of Carers UK. Fast-forward another year and I became chairman as the charity was gearing up for its fiftieth anniversary.

## LEARNING HOW EMPLOYERS HELP CARERS JUGGLING JOBS AND CARING

I quickly discovered that many care-givers are juggling their job and their caring responsibilities; and that one of the initiatives of Carers UK is *Employers for Carers* — an alliance of employers including British Gas, BT, KPMG, Sainsbury, the Metropolitan Police and others — who aspire to be great employers of care-givers. I am passionate about the work of Carers UK. Like the rest of my board and staff colleagues, I want to see a society which respects, values and supports carers. I want an end to carer isolation. No one should have to care alone. Given how many people are working and caring, reaching carers through their employers is one very important channel of communication. Supportive employers can help many carers to stay in work. Where that is possible, it is good for the employer, for the carer — and for the person being cared for and the rest of their family — both short term and for the future. I have a particular interest in this. I went half-time in my own job at Cranfield University School of Management, with a consequent 50% drop in salary and knock-on impact on pension pot, in order to help look after mum in her final couple of years. I don't regret that for a single moment.

## Becoming Mum's Carer

Despite all my previous experience and networks, I still struggled as a carer. My fitness routine was gradually abandoned. Progressively, I stopped accepting invitations to functions that weren't immediately necessary to my current work. Socialising declined. Anecdotal conversations with other carers, as well as research carried out by and for several of the carers' associations around the world, suggest my experience is very common. As one very successful executive with a top global company, who had quit her job to care for her mother, said to me: 'if you and I were struggling, as well-connected, reasonably well-off people, how much tougher is it for anyone with fewer friends and contacts or in a less fortunate material situation?' Her question has driven me on to complete this book.

*I want to see a society which respects, values and supports carers. I want an end to carer isolation. No one should have to care alone.*

More and more of us will be juggling work and looking after a loved one. I vividly recall walking through Oxford one Spring evening, several years ago. I was attending the Skoll World Forum on Social Enterprise. I was walking between events with an old friend and mentor Prof Kirk Hanson from California. Kirk is one of the world's leading business ethicists. I interrupted our conversation in order to make my nightly phone call to mum. I tried to make it the same time, 6 p.m., each night no matter where in the world I was. Kirk patiently waited for me to finish the call and then quietly commented: 'that is part of my next book!' I was confused. 'I thought your next book was about ethical dilemmas every manager will face?' I replied. 'It is', Kirk explained, 'and looking after elderly parents alongside your work is very much one of those!'

I was very fortunate. I could afford to take a 50% salary cut. Mum had wonderful neighbours: Jim and Pauline Harling, who popped across to see her every day and would alert me if anything untoward had happened when I was not there. I drastically reduced my overseas travel for work. When I did go abroad, we started to experiment with different respite care homes. Invariably, when I returned and collected mum, the home — unprompted — would say what a delight mum had been to look after; and they would be very pleased if she would like to stay. Mum, whilst unfailingly polite and appreciative to the care home staff, was always keen to get home. Although we did discuss different care options, I knew mum wanted to stay in her own home, if she possibly could — so that was my mission.

Eventually, mum needed 24/7 live-in care. Thanks to a chance introduction from a work colleague, I was connected to a small business *Miracle Workers* specialising in placing live-in professional care workers with clients. We were incredibly fortunate in meeting Ann Luff who looked after mum for most of her final 13 months. Ann's loving and calm presence lifted a great deal of the stress from me. I still made the 520 km round-trip from my home in London to Sheffield and back most weeks, but instead of food shopping and other domestic chores, it could be more about being a son, going through old photographs together, going out for meals and trips into Derbyshire, and reading poems and prayers.

My work on *Take Care* had a three-month hiatus when mum went in to a final, precipitate decline. I had always dreaded that I might be abroad for work and unable to get back in time. As it was, I realised mum was deteriorating, returned to Sheffield and then abandoned my return to London for meetings. It was good that I did. I was up all night with mum. The next morning, her long-standing GP who had only visited the day before, came back again and after examining mum, broke the news that she thought mum was dying. We both knew mum's wishes were to die at home. With the help of Ann, Jim and Pauline and wonderful district nurses, we were able to fulfil mum's wishes. My bedside vigil lasted

11 days and nights. Work colleagues were understanding and covered for me. It never occurred to me that my employer would be unsympathetic; but nor was I aware of formal policies for such circumstances. I simply intuited from my inchoate sense of the university culture. In truth, wild horses would not have dragged me away from mum, but it was still reassuring to feel the empathy and understanding of colleagues and employer. Once I did return to work some weeks after mum's death, I started to think not just about resuming work on *Take Care*, but also about how the university might turn informal custom and practice into a more structured Carers' Policy. My subsequent work on this book has, therefore, gone in parallel with some 'gentle nudging' (I am from Yorkshire remember!) of the University, as I will explain later on.

Looking after my mum in her later years, ensuring she could stay happily and safely in her own home and always have things to look forward to is the most important thing I have done in life and I imagine will remain so. I suspect a bereavement counsellor might consider, in some small way, *Take Care*, as my personal equivalent of 'H is for Hawk' — the acclaimed memoir of Helen Macdonald — a grief-stricken daughter who became obsessed with training a goshawk following her father's death, which won the Costa book of the year in 2015.

## ABOUT TAKE CARE

The book is written to be read straight through. However, for the time-pressed readers, there is an overview at the start of each section, and key take-aways at the end of each section. There are profiles of nearly 50 different employers and how they help working carers, spread through the text (see the box below).

| 3M | Multinational conglomerate | US | 123 |
|---|---|---|---|
| AbbVie | Pharmaceuticals | Israel | 72 |
| Accenture | Consulting | UK | 140 |
| Ajinomoto Group | Food | Japan | 111 |
| Associe International Inc | | UK | 161 |
| Astellas | Pharmaceuticals | Japan | 125 |
| Australian Bureau of Statistics | Government | Australia | 140 |
| Aviva Life | Insurance | UK | 87 |
| Be Inspired Films | Film-making | UK | 159 |
| BT | Telecommunications | UK/ international | 118 |
| Carnstone | Consultancy | UK | 157 |
| CBI Health Group | Health & care | Canada | 33 |
| Centrica | Energy | UK/North America | 173 |
| Cranfield University | Higher education | UK | 236 |
| Credit Suisse | Financial services | UK/ international | 143 |
| Deloitte, accountancy & consultancy | | Ireland | 125 |
| Emory University | Higher education | USA | 125 |
| Fannie Mae | Financial services | USA | 126 |
| FTI Consulting | Corporate communications | UK | 99 |
| Grosser Cleaning | Domestic services | Germany | 160 |
| GSK | Pharmaceuticals | international | 112 |
| Happy Consulting | Workplace well-being | UK | 160 |

| | | | |
|---|---|---|---|
| Harvard University | Higher education | USA | 124 |
| Hyde Housing | Social housing | UK | 112 |
| IBM | Multinational technology and consulting | | 39 |
| J&J | Pharmaceuticals | USA/ international | 88 |
| Johns Hopkins University | Higher education | USA | 83 |
| Listawood | Manufacturing | UK | 157 |
| Lloyds Banking Group | Financial services | UK | 133 |
| London Fire Brigade | Public sector | UK | 135 |
| Metropolitan Police | Public sector | UK | 82 |
| Ministry of Justice | Public sector | UK | 109 |
| Mitsubishi | | Japan | 111 |
| Network Rail | Transport infrastructure | UK | 75 |
| NHS Education Scotland | | | 80 |
| Otsuka | Pharmaceuticals | Japan | 115 |
| PWC | Accountancy & consulting | Australia/ international | 93 |
| Pukka Herbs | Food | UK | 159 |
| Sainsbury's | Retailing | UK | 116 |
| Scottish Courts & tribunal Service | Public sector | UK | 136 |
| Standard Life | Insurance | UK | 147 |
| Taisei | Construction | Japan | 125 |
| Thyssen Krupp | Engineering/manufacturing | Germany/ international | 112 |
| Unforgettable | Care | UK | 161 |
| Unilever | FMCG | UK/ international | 125 |

| Unipart | Logistics, supply chain, manufacturing and consultancy | UK/ international | 128 |
| Westpac | Financial services | Australia/ international | 113 |
| West Dunbartonshire Council | Public sector | UK | 110 |
| Wheatley Group | Social housing, community regeneration & care | Scotland | 134 |

## WHO SHOULD READ THIS BOOK?

Ambitiously, I have a number of target audiences for this book: employers, consultants, carer organisations around the world, Workplace Specialists in Business Representative Organisations, Business Development Organisations, Corporate Responsibility Coalitions and Work-Related Think-Tanks around the world, HR academics and professional associations and Governments. This is a diverse group but what they have in common is that they, like me, care about caring. And each organisation can take specific actions to improve its quality.

1. Employers
   - HR directors

   - Finance Directors/Chief Finance Officers – this is a bottom-line issue

   - heads of Diversity & Inclusion / team members

   - Corporate Responsibility / Sustainability directors

*Desired action*: Establish a carer policy if you don't yet have one; or review and improve if your organisation already provides some support for carers. Become part of a campaign to engage more employers.

2. Consultants in
   - Talent management and Human Resources
   - Diversity & Inclusion (D&I)
   - Corporate Responsibility and Sustainability
   - Work-life balance/Great Place to Work
   - EAP (Employee Assistance Programme) specialist providers
   
   *Desired action*: Add carer issues to your agenda with clients if caring for carers is not already included; or review and improve if you already have some support for carers in your agenda/offering to clients

3. Carer Advocacy and Support Organisations around the World
   *Desired action*: Consider adding working and caring to your activities e.g. creating an Employer for Carers type initiative

4. Workplace Specialists inside Business Representative Organisations, Business Development Organisations, Corporate Responsibility Coalitions and Work-Related Think-Tanks around the World
   *Desired action*: Add work and caring to your activities e.g. create an Employer for Carers type initiative in collaboration with your local carers organisations

5. Academics Specialising in Caring, Business School
International Human Resource Management
Faculty and HR Professional Associations (EG CIPD,
SHRM)
*Desired action*: Develop the case for why employers
should care for their employee carers, research
emergent employer practice, and add supporting work
and caring to your professional guidance and
International Human Resource Management (IHRM)
courses.

6. Governments and would-be Governments
*Desired action*: Politicians responsible for finance,
work and pensions, social affairs and health and
government ministries covering these topics.
Besides an important role as employers of many
working carers, a range of government policies and
initiatives can support employers to care for working
carers — or conversely make employer efforts less
impactful.

## UNDERSTANDING SUPPORT FOR WORKING CARERS AS A CORPORATE RESPONSIBILITY ISSUE

My friends and colleagues say I am an inveterate net-
worker and connector (some of them say any encounter
with me usually leads to some commitment on their part
to do something/meet someone etc.!). It is certainly
true that I have been a campaigner since before my childhood illness. I do like to spot and make connections for
positive impact. In this case, there is a very obvious
connection between my day job: as professor of Corporate

Responsibility at Cranfield University School of Management and my volunteering with Carers UK.

Corporate Responsibility is the responsibility which an organisation has for its Social, Environmental & Economic (SEE) impacts. A key part of corporate responsibility is the impact in the workplace: being a responsible employer — and ideally being a great employer.

Caring for working carers is like the missing jigsaw piece for several critical organisational strategies (**Diagram 1**). These include:

− creating a diverse and inclusive workplace

− talent attraction, retention and optimisation, especially in the context of an ageing workforce

− being a responsible employer

---

**Diagram 1: Caring For Carers: The Missing Jigsaw Piece.**

---

- boosting health and well-being in the workplace and especially, helping to tackle the taboo and stigma of mental ill-health

- being a great place to work

- building employee engagement and advocacy

- sustainably improving profitability through reducing costs and raising productivity

- building organisational resilience and future-proofing.

In a previous role as the first chairman of the UK's National Disability Council (NDC) from 1995 to 2000 (appointed by Parliament to work to end discrimination against disabled Britons), I saw at first-hand how organisations could adapt and develop to become responsible employers of those of us with a disability.

Coming in to Carers UK, it felt like employers of carers were where employers of disabled people had been twenty years ago, in terms of being integrated within mainstream workplace responsible business policies and practices. Back in 1996 when I started as the first chairman of the NDC, I persuaded KPMG to do some pro-bono work looking at the major Corporate Responsibility coalitions internationally. KPMG found that these coalitions were largely silent then on disability issues. A quick trawl of the websites of the major coalitions in 2016 showed them largely silent about employment and caring. Yet as societies age around the world, and as public expenditures come under increasing pressure, how employers can enable their employees to stay in work and simultaneously be effective carers is becoming a global issue. Since I started work on

*Take Care*, I have learnt of interest in Australia, Canada, Israel, New Zealand and Sweden to help employers be better at supporting their employee caregivers. My goal is that this book will inspire and help business organisations, Corporate Responsibility coalitions, carer associations, individual employers and social entrepreneurs, to champion caring for carers — and also provide practical guidance to individual employers around the world.

## HOW THIS BOOK IS ORGANISED

In Part 1, I argue that looking after a loved one is part of what it is to be human: caring is deeply ingrained in faith and philosophical traditions; and that caring will affect most of us at different points in our lives. I look at the Caring Journey and explain why employers and society needs to support better those who are working carers.

Synthesising my knowledge and experience of both corporate responsibility and caring, in Part 2, I set out a Seven Step framework — drawn from my book co-authored with Adrian Hodges, *Corporate Social Opportunity* — which responsible employers can follow to improve their support for working carers for the benefit of their businesses, as well as the carers they employ. I also show that even small employers can care for their carers.

In Part 3 Chapter 1, I describe how organisations can develop their operational practices even further, reaching the highest stages of corporate responsibility "maturity" to become "Champion" employers in their support for carers. In Part 3 Chapter 2, I consider how to support carers who are working as freelancers. In Part 3 Chapter 3, I suggest how governments and a range of other organisations and networks can build an enabling environment for more employers to take care of their working carers.


## A THEORY OF CHANGE TO BUILD A SOCIETY THAT RESPECTS, VALUES AND SUPPORTS CARERS

Carers UK has benefitted greatly from a collaboration with NESTA, the independent innovation foundation. NESTA puts a strong emphasis on supporting its partners to articulate a Theory of Change, that they are going to put into practice. A Theory of Change:

> *explains how a programme has an impact on its beneficiaries. It outlines all the things that a programme does for of its beneficiaries, the ultimate impact that it aims to have on them, and all the separate outcomes that lead or contribute to that impact.*

This has inspired me to consider my Theory of Change for *Take Care* and the international movement I hope we can unleash. The model is adapted and internationalised from the emerging *Theory of Change of Employers for Carers* (see **Diagram 2**).

I discuss how we can collaborate to implement the Theory of Change in my conclusion.

**Diagram 2: Theory of Change.**

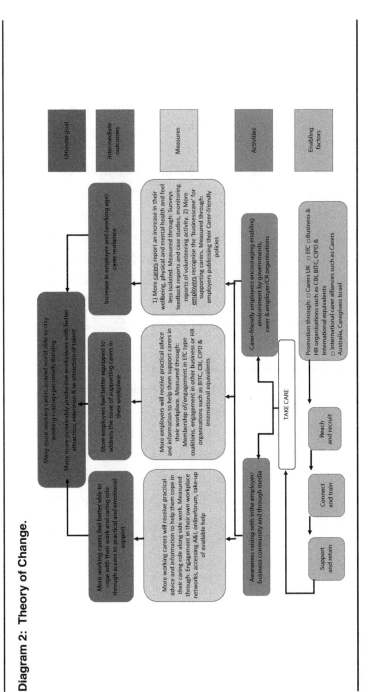

## WANTED: COMMITTED CITIZENS TO CHANGE THE WORLD

One thing that has powerfully resonated with me as I have researched and written *Take Care*, is the role of individual champions at all levels of organisations. Their stories are interspersed throughout the text. If ever I needed reminding of the famous observation of the late Margaret Mead: 'Never doubt that a small group of thoughtful, committed, citizens can change the world. Indeed, it is the only thing that ever has', my experience of the men and women I have interviewed and whose stories are told in the following pages, has done so. We need more of these 'committed citizens' — champions of carers in the workplace — to 'come out', tell their own stories and promote better help for working carers in individual workplaces and in wider society.

My hope is that, working in collaboration with responsible businesses and other partners, we can make support for working carers 'business as usual'. Many employers are already responding to the expectations and needs of more diverse, multi-generational workforces, with more customised work options. These can be easily stretched and adapted to meet the needs of working carers.

And yes, mum was pretty chuffed that she inspired this book!

# DISCLAIMER

I am chairman of Carers UK. All royalties from *Take Care* will go directly to Carers UK. I am deeply indebted to various colleagues in Carers UK for their help and advice as I researched and wrote *Take Care* – see acknowledgements. I very much hope that I have done justice to the experience and insights of Carers UK and our supporters; and also those of colleagues in a number of carer organisations around the world. Nevertheless, the views expressed in *Take Care* are my own and should not be assumed necessarily to represent the views of Carers UK.

# PART 1

---

## WHY CARE FOR CARERS?

# CHAPTER 1

## CARING AND CARERS

### INTRODUCTION

*Taking care of a loved one is part of the rhythm of life. The largest number of carers are those caring for a parent or other elderly relative, those looking after a partner with a long-term medical condition, and those caring for disabled sons, daughters or siblings. Ageing populations, advances in medical technology and pressures on state welfare budgets, all mean that in most parts of the world, the numbers of carers is increasing. This includes the numbers of those juggling work and caring. Work can be both a financial necessity and a respite for many carers. It can though also become part of a 'caring vicious circle'.*

Johnnie Walker — the veteran BBC radio disc jockey — and his wife Tiggy were on their honeymoon when Johnnie fell ill. He was diagnosed with a rare and very serious form of cancer. Overnight, Tiggy's own career as a successful producer of TV commercials had to be put on hold as she became Johnnie's carer, chauffeur, cook, contact with the outside world. Happily, Johnnie recovered. 12 years later, the roles were reversed when Tiggy developed breast cancer and Johnnie became Tiggy's carer. For some, like Johnnie and Tiggy, becoming a carer can happen in a flash — like a bolt of lightning in a clear blue sky.[1] Sometimes by contrast, you slowly, barely perceptibly at first, start helping a loved one with chores and daily routines, until you turn round one day and realise you have become a carer — even if you don't use that word.

Richard is an expat — a Briton living and working in Paris at the headquarters of a major French Pharmaceutical Company. His parents who live in the South-West of England are starting to become frailer and whilst they remain fiercely independent, Richard is noticing that on each visit he makes home, they need a bit more support. He is starting to consider what changes in how he does his job might be needed in the future to care for his parents as a 'distance carer'.


## WHO IS A 'CARER'?

The Guardian and Observer Newspapers' Style Guide defines a carer as:

> *An unpaid family member, partner or friend who helps a disabled or frail person with the activities of daily living; not someone who works in a caring job or profession. The term is important because carers are entitled to a range of benefits and services that depend on them recognising themselves as carers.*[2]

At Carers UK we say: 'A carer is someone of any age who provides unpaid support to family or friends who could not manage without this help due to illness, disability, mental ill-health or a substance misuse problem'.

The umbrella organisation Euro-carers defines a carer as a person who provides unpaid care to someone with a chronic illness, disability or other long-lasting health or care need, outside a professional or formal framework. In some parts of the world, the more common term in use is 'caregiver'.

Employers for Carers offers a working definition of Working carers as:

> *Employees with significant caring responsibilities that have a substantial impact on their working lives. These employees are responsible for the care and support of disabled, elderly or sick partners, relatives or friends who are unable to care for themselves.*[3]

## WHY SHOULD WE CARE ABOUT CARING?

### Caring is Becoming a Universal Human Experience

As the Rosalynn Carter quotation at the beginning of Take Care makes clear: Most of us will be involved in caring: as a giver, receiver or probably both at different stages of our lives. At different stages of my own life, I have already been all of those. I had to rely on my parents and other family members when I had a life-threatening bone disease and was immobilised in plaster of Paris for the best of a year. I saw my parents care for their parents; and I in turn cared for mine.

For many of us, this will include looking after someone else during our working lives. Caring is part of the human condition: It is part of what makes us human. It is integral to loving others and can bring great joy and emotional rewards. As one carer called Donna tweeted to me: 'Caring: the most isolating, emotionally + mentally draining, worry-filled, financially breaking but best job ever!'

The sheer scale and scope of caring, as well as the growth in carer numbers, illustrates how widespread and diverse the caring experience is becoming in our society. In the United Kingdom, for example, there are 6.5 million carers (58% women, 42% men). The majority are caring for parents, are aged 45–64 years, are juggling work and care, and are more likely to be women in this age group (one in four compared with one in six men). Men are more likely to be caring for partners, women more likely to care for parents and children. 1.4 million are caring over 50 hours/week, 4 million provide 1–19 hours care per week. Today's 6.5 million carers are projected to grow to 9 million by 2037.[4]

It is estimated that 20 million people across the European Union provide over 20 hours weekly of unpaid informal care work.[5] In the Netherlands, for example, data suggests that in 2014 over 4 million people (33% of Dutch adults) had provided some form of informal care in the year preceding. Informal care is interpreted broadly here, and includes things such as providing emotional support or helping with transport 10% of informal carers provide help only with emotional support or companionship. Many people help long-term (>3 months) but not intensively (maximum 8 hours/week). Roughly one in six informal Dutch carers provide help for more than 8 hours a week. Over 600,000 people provide help for more than 3 months and more than 8 hours/week. These figures exclude the 'usual help' which household members are expected to provide to each other.[6]

In the United States, there are an estimated 65 million caregivers. According to the US National Alliance for Caregiving (NAC), family caregivers provide an average of 20 hours of care per week, and for most, caregiving isn't limited to a few months, or even a year — NAC's research found that caregiving lasts an average of almost 5 years.[7] By 2020, one in six Americans will be over 65 years and more than one in three Americans will likely have eldercare responsibilities. In Australia, there are 2.6 million carers.[8]

According to Statistics Canada, in the 15 years from 1997, the number of Canadian caregivers increased by over 5 million, from 2.85 million in 1997[9] to over 8 million in 2012.[10] 8.1 million or 28% of Canadians were providing such care. Of this group, three-quarters (6.1 million) were in the workforce, representing 35% of employed Canadians. The number of Canadian seniors requiring care is projected to double between 2012 and 2031.[11]

Even in Scandinavia where there is a tradition of public social welfare provision, budget pressures are leading to increasing numbers of informal caregivers. As an important study from the influential Chartered Institute of Personnel and Development (CIPD) noted in 2016:

> *The relatively good level of state provision in*
> *place for eldercare in Denmark means that the*

*families of older people typically do not have to*
*arrange and manage care for them. Danish stud-*
*ies have shown that only a minority of elderly citi-*
*zens who need care rely on personal help from*
*their family members or other members of their*
*social networks, because the state provision is*
*comprehensive. However, some economists in*
*Denmark note that, in the longer term, the*
*Danish economy will also be under pressure*
*because of the ageing of the Danish population*
*and this trend will eventually bring pressure to*
*bear on the system as it currently stands.*[12]

The study goes on to argue: 'Providing help for older
workers with care responsibilities should be a priority for
employers'.

A survey conducted by the OECD in 2011, found that
around one in 10 adults in OECD countries were
involved in informal, typically unpaid family care.

Encouragement and support for voluntary caregivers is
included within the new United Nations Sustainable
Development Goals (SDG) adopted in September 2015.
SDG 5.4 is to:

*Recognise and value unpaid care and domestic*
*work through the provision of public services,*
*infrastructure and social protection policies and*
*the promotion of shared responsibility within the*
*household and the family as nationally*
*appropriate.*[13]

Chris Minett, Founder of Ageing Works (now part of
Mercer), talks of the 'seismic shift' that will be needed by

individuals and by employers, as many more of us are called upon to care for parents and other elderly relatives.

## The Challenges of Caring can Impact all Aspects of Life

Being a carer can be very rewarding, but caring can also have significant impacts on work, social and family life. Caring can also involve great sacrifice – and have physical, mental, social and financial costs. These costs can become negatively reinforcing: a kind of caring vicious circle. Reducing or giving up work generally means less money, which leads to a reduction in opportunities for a social life and increasing isolation, which in turn can impact negatively on physical and mental health (Diagram 1).

It is in the interests of carers themselves, those being cared for, employers and society at large, to tackle the caring vicious circle. No one group alone will be able to defeat the caring vicious circle. It will require

**Diagram 1: Caring Vicious Circle Nexus Diagram.**

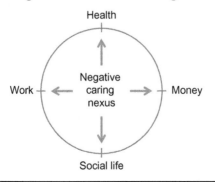

commitment and collaboration. Take Care emphasises the particular contributions that employers of all shapes and sizes can make.

'Caregiving is a nuanced issue; the intensive, short-term needs of caring for a terminally ill parent contrast greatly with the decades of on-going care required for a child with a disability. We need to recognise that different people need different accommodations in different situations,' says Stephen Shea, Senior Partner of the Accountants and Consultants at EY (Ernst & Young Global Limited) in Toronto, who chaired a panel on caring and carers for the previous Canadian Government of Stephen Harper.

## Caring Takes its Toll on Carer Health and Well-being

Finding time for yourself is hard and it's easy for your own health and well-being to become a low priority.

The most recent UK Census (2011) suggests that those providing over 50 hours of care per week are twice as likely to be in bad health compared with non-carers. The GP Patient Survey 2015 showed that whilst 51% of non-carers had a long-standing health condition, this rose to 63% of all carers and 70% of those caring for 50 hours or more. Carers' own experiences suggest that long-term back problems and mobility problems are caused by long-term physical stress, moving and handling without the right equipment or training. Anxiety and depression rates are high, with Carers UK's 2015 survey of carers providing significant care — 77% recording anxiety and 83% recording depression since becoming a carer.[14] 71% of employee carers report loneliness and social isolation. Carers UK work with carers for our *Alone and Caring Report* found:

- 8 in 10 (83%) carers have felt lonely or socially isolated as a result of their caring responsibilities.

- 57% of carers have lost touch with friends and family as a result of caring and half (49%) of carers say they have experienced difficulties in their relationship with their partner because of their caring role.

- 38% of carers in full-time employment have felt isolated from other people at work because of their caring responsibilities.

- Carers who have reached breaking point as a result of caring are twice as likely to say that they are socially isolated because they are unable to leave the house and are also more likely to have experienced depression as a result of caring.[15]

*Juggling caring and work responsibilities is becoming increasingly difficult for carers, employers...and economies.*

## WORKING CARERS

In Israel, it is estimated 1:4 employees are also caregivers. In Australia, it is estimated that 1:8 (12%) of the working populations are carers. 60% of the estimated 65 million US caregivers were employed at some point in the past year while also caregiving. There are currently 6.1 million employed Canadians, or 35% of the workforce, providing care to a family member or friend. Most employed caregivers spend 9 hours or less per week caring, but many (24%) are spending up to 30 hours – and some even more. The recipients of care are primarily seniors, and most caregivers are 45 years and older, often talented and experienced employees possessing deep company or industry knowledge. These are key contributors to an organisation and to the Canadian economy broadly — people employers don't want to see exit the workforce.[16]

About 4.3 million out of 6.5 million carers of the United Kingdom are of working age – but only 3 million are in work. Men are more likely to be working full-time and caring for their partner. Women are more likely to be working part-time. In an average, UK workforce, 1:9 employees will also have caring responsibilities. An estimated 2.3 million people in the United Kingdom have given up work at some point to care and 3 million have cut working hours. Many of these employees – the 45–64 years old, often at the peak of their careers – are among organisations' most skilled people.

As the pension age increases, the likelihood of caring during working life, is increasing. Employers, through Carers UK forum and through others like CIPD, are reporting increasing numbers of employers seeing stress, ill-health and difficulty in juggling work and care amongst their employees and rate this as one of the fastest growing issues in their workforce. Despite the challenges of combining care with employment, 400,000 people are doing a full working week alongside long hours of care (20 hours or more). As social welfare nets decline, it is likely that these numbers will become increasingly similar pro-rata in other countries (Diagram 2).

---

**Diagram 2: Caring and Working Across the European Union.**

**Eurofound** — Caring for elderly or disabled relatives among people in employment, EU28

*(At least once a week, by age and gender, 2011/12)*

|  | Male | | Female | |
|---|---|---|---|---|
|  | Carer | Non-carer | Carer | Non-carer |
| 18-24 | 11% | 89% | 10% | 90% |
| 25-34 | 7% | 93% | 10% | 90% |
| 35-49 | 12% | 88% | 18% | 82% |
| 50-64 | 18% | 82% | 22% | 78% |

Coordinating the Network of EU Agencies 2015

**Eurofound** — Providing care at least once or twice a week

|  |  | Non-carer | Working carer | Other carer |
|---|---|---|---|---|
| Cluster 1: | Sweden, Denmark, Finland | 89% | 8% | 3% |
| Cluster 2: | Austria, Belgium, Germany, Netherlands, France, Luxembourg | 86% | 9% | 5% |
| Cluster 3: | United Kingdom, Ireland | 82% | 10% | 8% |
| Cluster 4: | Italy, Greece, Portugal, Spain, Cyprus, Malta | 86% | 7% | 7% |
| Cluster 5: | Poland, Hungary, Czech Republic, Slovakia, Croatia, Slovenia | 83% | 10% | 7% |
| Cluster 6: | Latvia, Lithuania, Estonia | 81% | 11% | 8% |
| Cluster 7: | Romania, Bulgaria | 85% | 8% | 7% |
| EU28: |  | 85% | 9% | 6% |

Coordinating the Network of EU Agencies 2015

| | | Non-carer | Working carer | Other carer |
|---|---|---|---|---|
| Cluster 1: | Sweden, Denmark, Finland | 95% | 3% | 2% |
| Cluster 2: | Austria, Belgium, Germany, Netherlands, France, Luxembourg | 92% | 5% | 3% |
| Cluster 3: | United Kingdom, Ireland | 89% | 5% | 6% |
| Cluster 4: | Italy, Greece, Portugal, Spain, Cyprus, Malta | 89% | 5% | 6% |
| Cluster 5: | Poland, Hungary, Czech Republic, Slovakia, Croatia, Slovenia | 88% | 7% | 5% |
| Cluster 6: | Latvia, Lithuania, Estonia | 85% | 9% | 6% |
| Cluster 7: | Romania, Bulgaria | 89% | 5% | 6% |
| EU28: | | 90% | 5% | 5% |

**Caring several times a week or more often**

*Source*: Reproduced with kind permission of Robert Anderson, Eurofound: European Foundation FOR THE IMPROVEMENT OF LIVING AND WORKING CONDITIONS.

## CARING, REDUCING OR GIVING UP WORK AND IMPACT ON FAMILY FINANCES

Giving up work partially or altogether, will have both immediate and long-term negative impacts on the carer's finances: an immediate drop in income and frequently also eating into savings; but also the carer's eventual pension pot will be much smaller.

Having to juggle work with caring duties can lead to significantly lower earnings, as people reduce their working hours, pass up promotion and overtime or even quit. This also has a knock-on effect on the carer's pension funds. According to 2016 research by Age UK and Carers UK, pension savings of those receiving Carer's Allowance are 90% smaller than the average. Many feel forced to give up their own paid work, finding the juggling too much to bear on top of the strain of looking after someone they love.

Age UK and Carers UK concluded: 'But when they do stop working the financial loss they incur is huge and often has consequences for the rest of their lives. It is morally wrong that people who do the right thing by becoming a carer should so seriously undermine their own financial security as a result'.

An additional £5.3 billion would flow back into the economy if carers could stay in the workplace until normal retirement age.

From the employer's perspective, many of the people giving up work to care, will be in the 45–64 age range — which in many organisations equates to the peak years of experience and productivity.

According to the AARP (formerly the American Association of Retired Persons) Public Policy Institute, quoted in Juggling Life, Work and Caregiving, American working caregivers often have to alter their working situation, to the detriment of long-term career advancement and financial security:

> '68% of caregivers have had to make work accommodations, such as taking time off, coming in late, leaving early, refusing a promotion, reducing working hours, changing jobs or quitting. Low-income employees, minorities and women are most likely to make work accommodations to care for older relatives. Cutting back on hours or quitting can hurt earnings as well as health insurance, social security benefits and contributions to retirement plans.

*19% of retirees stopped working earlier than
planned because of caregiving, with significant
loss of income: Female caregivers aged 50 + who
stop working to care for a parent lose an average
of $324,044 in wages and benefits over the course
of their lives: Male caregivers aged 50 + lose an
average of $283,716.*

*Caregivers who work are more likely than their
non-caregiving colleagues to have health challenges and report fair or poor health in general'.*[17]

A 2016 survey amongst over 3,600 employees at eight
Israeli employers conducted by Caregivers Israel found
that:

*85% of respondents said their work schedule was
disrupted by caring*

*81% reported absences from work due to their
caring responsibilities*

*19% had thought about changing their job*

*and 13% had declined a promotion because of
juggling job and caring.*[18]

### TRIGGERS TO GIVING UP WORK

Carers New Zealand says there are a number of triggers
that may see employees who have caring responsibilities
consider leaving. These include:

*An increase in their level of caring*

*An increase in their workload*

*A change in working hours, shift patterns or
rosters*

*The start of caring responsibilities, which can be a
stressful time for families*

*A sudden health trauma or accident in the family,
or a distressing diagnosis*

*Lack of support or understanding from managers
or colleagues*

*Inability to work flexibly*

*Struggling to find (and afford) reliable relief care
during work hours.*

*In most cases, therefore, making it easier to carry
on working – even if it is part-time – will be in
everyone's interest.*[19]

## CARING IS INVALUABLE BUT ECONOMICALLY UNDERVALUED

A 2009 study estimated the imputed economic cost to replace family caregivers in Canada with paid workforce (at current market rates and usual employee benefits) totalled $25 billion.[20] This equates to 14% of the total healthcare expenditures in Canada.[21]

According to Family Caregiver Alliance,[22] there are approximately 65 million family caregivers in the United States providing care for parents, relatives, spouses and children. The Valuing the Invaluable: 2015 Update[23] reports the estimated economic value of their unpaid contributions was approximately *$470 billion in 2013*, up from an estimated *$450 billion in 2009*.[24] That is more than twice what is spent nationwide on nursing homes and paid home-care combined.

An August 2015 study by the consulting firm Deloitte calculated that the replacement cost of informal caring in Australia would be Australian $60 billion p.a. or 3.8% of Australian gross domestic product (GDP vs. Aus $40.8 billion in 2010).[25] Carers New Zealand estimate that the benefits to the New Zealand economy from unpaid care work probably accounts for around 5% of GDP, or NZ $10.8 billion a year.[26]

The economic value of the contribution made by carers in the United Kingdom is now £132 billion/year, almost double its value in 2001 (£68 billion).[27] £132 billion is close to the total annual cost of health spending in the United Kingdom, which was £134.1 billion[28] in the year 2014–2015. It is more than the market value of HSBC Holdings or Visa PLC.[29]

The 2015 UK figure is 7% higher than the figure for 2011. This is mostly because carers are providing more hours of care (82%), and partly due to the increased hourly cost of paid home-care (18%). The figures mean that, in 2015, the value of the contribution made by the UK's carers saves the public purse enormous sums every week, day and hour of the year:

- £2.5 billion/week

- £362 million/day

- £15.1 million/hour.[30]

## WHO CARES? CARER ARCHETYPES

By far the largest group of carers are those caring for an elderly parent or other elderly relative. As populations age across the world, this will become even more pronounced with a growing number of 'young old' caring for the 'old old'. Often, an 'old-old' husband and wife will be caring for each other. Over 80s carers are a fast-growing component of carers in a number of countries. My Mum was principal carer for my Dad up to his death aged 86 years. Mum was then 88 years. One reason why populations are growing is because more of us are living longer, thanks to advances in medical technology.

Similarly, more people with severe disabilities are surviving and becoming adults. Significant numbers of carers are looking after a disabled son or daughter. Siblings may suddenly face a double-whammy — needing to start looking after their elderly parents, and also their disabled brother or sister who previously their parents had been caring for, but are no longer able to do so. 'What if I can no longer care for the person I love?' asked Bruce Bonyhady, then Chairman of the Australian National Disability Insurance Agency.[31] This will become an increasingly common fear.

A third significant group of carers are those caring for their spouse/partner. This may be for short, intensive bursts as in the case of Johnnie and Tiggy Walker quoted above, or it may involve looking after the partner for several decades if it is a long-term medical condition.

There is also a smaller, fourth quadrant of people caring for friends and neighbours although typically they will be caring less intensively, less intimately than the first

**Diagram 3: Carer Segment.**

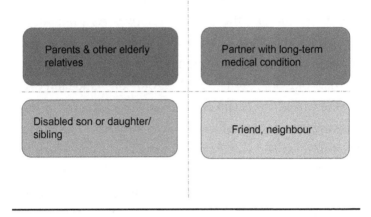

three quadrants; and children/young people caring for a parent or another, older relative (see **Diagram 3**).

Carers may also be defined by the long-term medical condition of the person they are caring for such as carers of people living with dementia or with mental illness, or with an addiction. Another carer segmentation is by communities of identity of the carers themselves such as BME (Black and Minority Ethnic) carers or LGBT (lesbian, gay, bisexual or trans) carers.

TAKE-AWAY

Most of us will look after a loved during our lives. Many of us will do so several times. Caring can be one of the most rewarding things we ever do; but it can also have physical, mental, social and financial costs. Early self-identification as a carer and timely access to relevant information and support, can make caring much easier and more rewarding.

# CHAPTER 2

# THE CARING JOURNEY: DESPATCHES FROM THE FRONTLINE

*Caring is a very personal experience and every carer's journey is unique. There are, however, frequently experienced stages on the 'caring journey'. Working carers can be supported or undermined, as they pass through these stages.*

For some of us, it is very sudden and obvious when our Caring Journey starts: A loved one has a bad accident or is diagnosed with a serious illness. In many other cases, however, caring creeps up on us. At first, our relationship with the person we are caring for barely changes. Slowly, almost imperceptibly, we start to help with chores. Gradually this increases. Whilst each Caring Journey will be unique, there are usually some common stages or milestones (see **Diagram 1**).

— Pre-caring — the 'Will-bes'.

— New to caring: When we first start to look after someone — the 'Newbies'.

**Diagram 1: Caring Journey.**

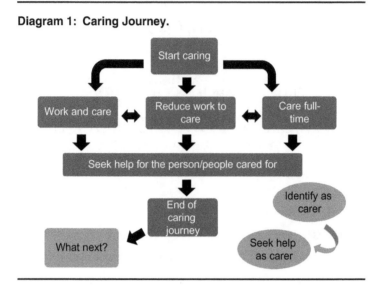

— Gradual realisation of role: When we first need to seek external help/advice from a health or other professional on behalf of the person being looked after, as more help is needed: the 'More-bes'.

— Acceptance of role and a more proactive/involved role: When paid care has to be introduced into the home of the person being cared for, when you become part of a caring circle — the 'Circlers'.

— If you move in with the person you are looking after, or they move into your home.

— If you bring in live-in paid carers or when the person you are caring for has to move in to a residential home.

— End of life caring vigil — the 'Vigilers'.

- When the Caring Journey is over (either because the person cared for has recovered or they have died) — the 'post-carers'.

In practice, some carers will miss out on some stages entirely, may experience them in a very different order and in a non-linear way, and the pressures of caring can vary with the stages. The carer may, for example, experience much greater pressures and stress before they access paid careworkers to help them. Some stages may be simultaneously experienced, i.e., a carer has understood a condition and is managing to care, but a new condition develops that leads them into a whole new area of caring — making them new to that particular area of caring.

Diagram 1 deliberately leaves 'floating' the stage at which a person self-identifies as a carer. For some people it may be very early in their Caring Journey. Some may never think of themselves as a carer. They remain hidden or invisible carers. In my case, it was several years in after my dad had died, and when I had already been travelling weekly from London to Sheffield for almost three years. (see introduction page xxxix). Often the carer's own view of their status may be complicated by the perception of the person they are caring for, who may not accept that they need help or that they are being cared for. It is harder to accept that you are indeed now a carer, if the person cared for is in denial!

Emily Holzhausen, the long-serving and highly respected Director of Policy and Public Affairs at Carers, UK, has distilled insights from colleagues and outside experts to reflect on the stages of the Caring Journey (see box below).

## Stages of the Caring Journey[32]

1.  Pre-caring: Horizon scanning — 'what happens if'? This group is not currently caring, but it will be on their horizon in a few years time or even a few months time.

    This group would primarily be those aged 45+ in relation to their parents. This might also include some partners/spouses and some siblings/close relatives.

2.  New to Caring Starting caring without knowledge of the future, and what it will entail. No overt realisation of the caring role. Would not typically call themselves a 'carer'. At this stage, feelings can be characterised as 'bewildered', 'lost', 'don't really know what needs to be done', 'don't know where to find the information'. There is also some element of them 'not knowing what they need to know', i.e. not knowing what questions to ask. Carers with great experience use their hindsight to say 'I wish I'd done this/asked that/ prepared for this'. There is also some lack of wishing to think too far into the future — just as those newly diagnosed with a degenerative condition don't wish to join support groups — they don't want to see the future of their disability. What carers need at this stage will depend on the caring situation:

    —   Horizon planning: Looking at what might be needed in the future.

    —   Immediate planning: 'I need a care service/something to keep mum safe'.

    —   Very involved activity: 'I'm responsible for his care now he's coming out of hospital and they've given me this plan and I don't know what I'm supposed to be doing with it'. The majority will be caring at a distance and caring for a parent.

3. Gradual realisation of the role: This is where the carer is starting to realise that they are the person that is starting to arrange, support or do the tasks necessary to support the disabled/ill person. They will typically have started to look for information about the condition and learn much more about it. They will not necessary call themselves a carer. Their feelings will be characterised by frustration, anger in some cases, still feeling lost and at sea. However, they are starting to build up a body of knowledge and will be ready to go for more in-depth information. They will be starting to make more decisions/support more decisions around care. They know more about what they need to know and can reflect back on what they might have done differently. Some carers might skip this stage entirely.

4. Acceptance of the role and a much more proactive, in-depth role By now, some people will be far more cognisant of their role, some will accept their role, some will be angry and frustrated at having to be a carer. Some will continue not to recognise what they are doing as a carer.

At this stage, they are much clearer about what they want and need and more direct about it. They will be able to look back at the earlier stages of their caring journey and reflect upon what they would have done differently. They will be starting to become more expert in particular areas of caring. They will typically need more specific and complex advice. They will have many more advice interventions needed because of the complexity of support that they need.

This stage of caring includes a much more involved role of caring, up to full-time caring.

5.  When caring comes to an end. *End of life care* is defined from around two years before a person may die, but in services terms and what people commonly think of as end of life, this is far shorter. Caring coming to an end may also entail someone recovering, getting better, or being able to manage with almost no support at all. Caring coming to an end where the person dies is characterised in the shorter term by a more intense period of support and concern. The focus is on making someone have the best life possible towards the end of life. Here the intervention, worry, etc. can be far more intense. Usually little pre-planning has been done about what happens when caring does end, however, some of the more technical areas such as LPA (lasting power of attorney), Wills, etc. legal documents are all critically important to be in order.

6.  After caring: This can be divided into two perhaps three periods. The first is immediately after caring has ended and when someone has died, this can be accompanied by a great deal of work dealing with affairs. It can be accompanied by a sense of loss of role and a 'vacuum' after intense periods of caring as well as bereavement. The second stage of after caring is when all the affairs have been completed, but the area of loss of role has not been attended to. Some people may, at this stage, move onto other areas, e.g. find new interests, new volunteering roles — some of which is helping other carers, some is completely different, taking on new paid work, changing jobs, moving house, etc. Others remain trapped in an area of loss where some of the negative aspects of caring endure: low income, poverty, depression and physical ill-health, loss of friendships, isolation and a loss of sense of purpose.

Major transitions that affect caring: This is not a stage in itself, in the caring journey, but is something that would cause a carer to leap from one stage to another, faster. These major transitions include:

- Caring that impinges on ability to work — putting the carer at risk of a significant work transition, i.e., sickness, time off, flexible working or leaving altogether

- Hospital discharge and in-patient admission

- Major treatment intervention (either needing more care, or requiring less care, e.g., being sectioned or a CTO (compulsory treatment order)).

- Large or significant events, e.g., fall, relapse, episode.

## WHAT EMPLOYERS NEED TO KNOW ABOUT THE CARING JOURNEY

For people caring and working, there can be additional, significant stages:

— when you have to seek help at work;

— when you have to go part-time or give up work entirely.

Employers can play an important role in supporting working carers on their journey, as these examples illustrate.

### Individual Employee Carer Profiles

With careful planning and flexibility from carer and employer, some carers can resume work, even with continuing caring responsibilities, as Helen Johnson's experience, described in the preface shows.

### Adriano De Gennaro, Aviva

Adriano De Gennaro works as a Customer Service Manager within Protection in the Bristol office of the insurer Aviva. His son Freddie is 8 years old. Unfortunately, he has life-threatening and life-limiting health issues. Freddie's complex needs started when he was only 3 weeks old when he contracted meningitis. Since then every year Freddie has regressed in heath. So for all of his time working for Aviva, De Gennaro has had to deal with uncertainties and worries. His wife Justine is Freddie's full-time carer as De Gennaro works full time. The family receive some respite: They stay at the local Children's Hospice South West 14 days a year.

Freddie needs 24/7 care. Over the past year Freddie has suffered from eight seizures, six of these while his father has been in the office. 'It's hard to explain what I feel like when I receive the call and I have to dash out of the office, not just for Freddie but the guilt I have for leaving my team and department. There have been times when he has stopped breathing and the Air ambulance has been called out on a couple occasions'.

Happily, De Gennaro has enjoyed excellent support from Aviva: 'I have been really supported by my past and current managers who have been fantastic to me. The care, support and consideration of my well-being have been great and from a personal perspective I couldn't ask for more. Being a manager myself I need to be in the office for my team, so being allowed to leave at short notice isn't ideal but the company and people understand why. I have needed to take my full quota of family emergency days on an annual basis due to having to attend appointments at Great Ormond Street Hospital in London. Freddie's sibling Joseph who is 11 in March 2017 loves his times in the ambulances and thinks its great fun, if I'm honest though he has seen too much pain and been through a lot for his age, this is an added strain and worry on my family and Joseph has had to attend counselling sessions due to this'.

Aviva's Employee Assistance Programme (EAP) has been a fantastic benefit for the De Gennaro family: 'Due to my experience it's easy for me to promote the EAP within my team and quite a few of them have used it. It really helps to have a Blackberry so that I do not feel guilty; it means I can keep in touch with what is going on in the office. I have a fantastic lead that has a lot of experience and I can rely on him, my peers will also muck in and help where required'.

'In my team a few people including my manager have met Freddie, he is pretty cute (obviously takes after his mother!!) and is one for the ladies, he loves a cuddle and tickle (Just like his dad). Meeting him has helped others understand my situation and the support and questions is sometimes overwhelming, this really helps me cope when I am having a bad day. Last week I took Freddie for an assessment at Great Ormond Street, most of my team and all of my peers asked me how we got on, that is special to me'.[33]

As Amy Goyer, the family and caregiving expert at the US AARP writes in her book *Juggling Life, Work, and Caregiving*:

'Working caregivers are employed in every industry and at every level. We are self-employed and work for a variety of companies, from small local businesses to large global conglomerates. We work as CEOs, teachers and receptionists. We work on Wall Street, in restaurants, and on construction sites. We work from home, offices, stores and factories. We interact with people on the phone; we use computers and video conferencing; and we serve customers face-to-face. We work full-time, part-time, and flexitime, night shifts, day shifts, and every combination in between. Some of us travel for our jobs. Working caregivers are everywhere, though you may not know it. Some of us are open at work about our caregiving roles but others keep it to themselves. Those who don't disclose their caregiving situations may do so for personal reasons, but many keep quiet because they are concerned about repercussions at work'.

A 2015 Survey for Carers, UK found that 60% of working carers were worried about their ability to remain in work over the next year.[34]

## A Story of Two Work Places: Support versus Barriers for Working Caregivers

Suzette Brown is one such working caregiver. For five years, she was the primary caregiver for her mother with Alzheimer's, while working full-time. Recently, she wrote about the challenges she faced and about why caregivers need paid leave.[35]

Suzette Brown worked full-time whilst caring for her mother with Alzheimer's, in an assisted living facility (ALF) for five years from 1999 to 2004. Suzette was a schools administrator in the US state of Virginia. She explains 'the employees and my bosses I worked with at that time were wonderful, understanding and very supportive of me. My caregiving duties were made much easier by understanding and sympathetic bosses. I will always be grateful to them for this time'. I still have the plaque that was given to me stating: 'A Wild, Wacky, Wonderful Woman Works Here'.

A few months after starting to care, Brown and her family moved because of her husband's job. She took a new job. It became apparent fairly quickly that this particular job would not permit her to leave to simply 'take care of my mother' as readily as the previous employer. Co-workers were nowhere near as understanding.

'I could feel the resentment from certain personnel — and it escalated to the point where my phone calls were screened. I started being asked if I was on a 'personal or work-related call' and 'who was I speaking to'. Then I was informed that my personal calls were not allowed at work, even after I explained that they were regarding my mother'.

'I didn't want to explain my Mom's condition to any of my bosses at work. I honestly felt it was none of their business. Mom's privacy and dignity were two things I vowed to keep sacred, for her. I explained to the bosses the bare minimum, simply letting them know that my mother had been diagnosed with Alzheimer's by medical professionals, that I was her DPOA (Designated Power of Attorney) and caregiver. I let them know that at least now she was in an ALF, safe and taken care of, but from time to time certain episodes occurred that called for me to leave and be by Mom's side'.[36]

## Work versus Caring: The Need for Balance

In 2003, Brown could no longer manage both work and caring, and switched professions, to one that would allow her to balance her role as caregiver with her duties in the workplace. Brown subsequently wrote about her experiences in her book *Alzheimer's Through My Mother's Eyes* (2013).[37]

It can be exhausting to juggle your job and caring for a loved one: splitting yourself in two, often seeking to balance conflicting priorities, feeling you need to be in several places at once. Sometimes, the needs of the person you are caring for, means it is no longer practical to combine work and caring, and you have to give up work. On the other hand, many carers describe their job as a form of respite from caring — a welcome opportunity to be absorbed in other things than the needs of the person cared for. For long-term carers in particular, news from work can also be a valuable source of conversation topics with a loved one who is house-bound or institutionalised.

This idea of work as respite and solace is well-illustrated by the case of Nedhal Sahar in Toronto, Canada.

## Nedhal Sahar

(Financial Controller, CBI Health Group)[38]

Caring for an older sister, who has multiple health conditions

*Credit*: Canadian Home Care Association.

Nedhal moved from her native Iraq to Canada as a skilled worker in 1999; and shortly afterwards joined what is now CBI Health Group, as an accounting supervisor. She was promoted to her current role as a financial controller five years later.

In 2009, Nedhal's sister, who is completely disabled and dependant, moved in with her and her husband. 'When my sister came to my house, I welcomed her. But it was the hardest time because there was no plan for me to have something like this', says Nedhal. 'The impact was really huge — emotionally and personally with work responsibilities'. Now, Nedhal's health is also affected. But to Nedhal, her sister's well-being is a priority. 'Looking at her, I think it is not her fault. I just keep on going even though I have health issues now', she says.

'She is the priority in everything. I feel like I have to be strong because otherwise I will collapse'. Through these difficult times, the support Nedhal receives from her co-workers at CBI Health Group has made a difference. 'When I hear good words from colleagues, it helps a lot. Just hearing 'Let me know if you need any help' helps a lot'.

Although CBI Health Group is a relatively large organisation (almost 10,000 employees across Canada) and over 40 years old, it does not have a formal carers policy or formal written policies for flexible or home-working. Rather these are part of the CBI Health Group empowering culture. Acknowledging the personal commitments in the life of CBI employees, accommodating and supporting them is part of CBI values.

Nedhal has agreed both flexible and some home-working (1 day/week) with her boss, one of the Vice-Presidents (Finance). Similarly, she has approved flexible working for her reports such as for an Indian man who was given extended leave and remote working facilities so he could return to India for the funeral of his mother and to deal with family affairs whilst there. Nedhal's emphasis on organisational culture is well-validated: in 2010, CBI Health Group was chosen as one of the 10 most admired corporate cultures in Canada.

When I spoke to Nedhal and asked for her advice to other working carers, her words struck a powerful chord with me:

> *Balance! Make sure you find the balance between caring and work and still enjoying a good life yourself. If*

*you fall over, you won't be able to care for your loved one. You have got to take care of yourself, in order to care for others.*

## When Carers Give up Work

Often, the personal circumstances of the carer or the person cared for; or the nature/location of the carer's employment, means that giving up work is the only, or the preferred choice. This was the position that James Ashwell found himself in.

### James Ashwell

When James Ashwell, then an Accenture strategy consultant, realised the extent of his mum's dementia, he and his brother moved back home to Birmingham, and promised her she wouldn't have to go through it alone.

Keeping this promise as his mum declined steadily over the next five years is the hardest thing James has ever done.

'Mum's increasingly disorganised behaviour and moments of sadness were something I learned to live with as a teenager, blaming her hormones, tiredness or simple forgetfulness. I feel terrible when I remember how irritated I got when she developed a habit of chewing repetitively with her mouth empty. When she picked me up from army cadets one day and started driving home on the wrong side of the road it dawned on me that there was more to it. We knew she was ill, but none of my siblings realised just how far her illness had progressed until 17 January 2006 — just before I turned 25. I received a phone call at work informing me that Dad had died suddenly a few hours previously. I put on my jacket, walked out the office and never returned.

Mum and Dad had been happily married since 1968. They were a good team. Dad worked extremely hard and, aged 64, he was looking forward to retiring and enjoying his sunset years with Mum. Maybe that's why he couldn't bring himself to tell us that Mum had been diagnosed with fronto-temporal dementia in 2003. He played it down, which wasn't too difficult because by then we'd all left home. I was a strategy consultant, my brothers were a doctor and an estate agent, and my sister was at medical school.

## Reaching Breaking Point

Dad's death changed everything in my life. Once I'd got back with Mum, it was clear that her condition had worsened considerably, compounded no doubt by grief. I was a gung-ho 25 year old and didn't have a clue what caring for a mum with dementia might entail. I was very fortunate to have siblings all prepared to help practically and financially. My brother Mark moved back home, too, which was just as well because those first few years were absolute hell. The first time I took Mum to the memory clinic, she dressed nicely, looked lovely and answered all the questions in the Mini Mental State Examination surprisingly well, but I was falling apart. I had a thousand questions for the doctor — including 'Is she going to die?' — and only 5 minutes of allotted time to ask them. In fact, I felt so overwhelmed that I burst into tears in front of the doctor. Eventually Mark and I did what most other carers do; we learnt to muddle through each day as best we could, always mindful that at least we had each other. How, I wondered, did people cope on their own? The toughest part was the lack of sleep. Mum got days and night mixed up, and we'd find her packing suitcases for an imaginary holiday at 3 a.m., or getting dressed for a lunch date at 4am.

Sometimes Mark and I didn't sleep much for a week and the stress and tiredness took their toll as they do with many families. One night we had a fight about nothing — we actually punched each other — which was horrible, but looking back I can see that the pressures were simply too much for both of us. This trauma forced us to start coming up with creative ways to make life more manageable. I remember tying string to Mum's bedroom door and putting it on my finger so I'd know if she left her room in the night! Looking back, it seems silly. But at the time, I genuinely didn't know what else I could do or where I could go for help. That's how it feels when we're under such stress. Now I have a pretty good understanding of the Caring Journey. Back then, I had no idea what the journey entailed and I wish I had because it would have made it so much easier.

## Improvising in the Carer's New World
We also applied our imaginations to making life better for Mum. We quickly realised that if Mum wasn't going to spend

all day sat staring at the TV, we needed to find new ways to keep her busy and give her a sense of purpose. If only we could find ways to bring her back. We wanted more than anything to see her face light up, and those moments when she looked happy or excited, however brief, became precious.

Mum and I worked together on a bucket list and did everything on it. Including going to Venice where Mum did horse-riding for the very first time. But the dementia journey is long, and even if you can afford special trips and outings, you can't spend every day doing them. We soon discovered that visiting garden centres or going to McDonalds for milk shakes (even if she did insist on walking through the drive thru!) brought Mum pleasure too, as did jigsaws, jewellery-making, drawing and colouring books — although we all fervently wished we could find some that weren't designed for children.

Mum declined steadily during the five years I was caring for her, gradually losing the ability to do most things for herself. But there were four siblings, and together we were fortunate enough to be able to pay for extra support from professional careworkers to help us out when things got really tough. And we still had many happy, hilarious moments with her, right to the end of her life. Community helped me — meeting other carers and realising I was not alone.

She died peacefully at home on 17 February 2011, a few hours after I turned 30. She was aged just 67. If there is such a thing as a good death, I'd like to think that she had it. This may not be possible for everyone, she had only one hospital admission. Looking back, I realised how lucky I was to have had a mum who gave everything for her children. That's why I wanted to give something back. I recognised how much I'd learned from other carers of people with dementia, as we shared our efforts not only to cope with the practical aspects of the condition but to seize every opportunity to connect, however fleetingly, with our loved ones as we knew them. Ultimately, I discovered how passionately I hold the belief that it is possible to cope with dementia and how motivated I was to help other people discover products and services which could really help them'.[39]

James went on to found Unforgettable in 2015, bringing together specialised products, practical advice and a supportive community to help those affected by memory loss and dementia. (*See Part 2 — SMEs and caring for carers page 161*).

So many aspects of James's story resonated with me. Bursting into tears in front of the doctor at the Memory Clinic. Discovering the pleasure of visits to garden centres. Finding colouring books for adults — the precision of my mum's artwork remained formidable to the end. The slow decline in ability to do things for herself. The sense of the good death at home. The sense of mums who gave everything for their children.

## THE "SANDWICH GENERATION": GROWTH IN CARING RESPONSIBILITIES FOR PARENTS AND CHILDREN

IBM's Vivien Kwok has experienced both the very sudden onset of caring and the slow, gradual build-up of more and more caring.

I joined IBM as part of the PwC Consulting acquisition in 2002 and have worked as a Project Manager in different areas, including BT&IT (Business Transformation and IT), Strategic Outsourcing and HR Global Mobility.

I have three children, born in 2007, 2009 and 2014. I was thrown into the maelstrom, which is the lot of the sandwich generation when my mother, who had helped with caring for my two older daughters whilst I worked, was diagnosed with terminal cancer in 2012. It seemed as if overnight my mother's and my roles reversed. We were given a bad prognosis of two to three months, and determined to make the most of the time I had remaining with my mother, I called my manager the next day and said I was going to take all my vacation, effective immediately, and then take unpaid leave once it runs out. By that stage my mother required assistance with walking and basic tasks such as bathing and changing, not to mention arranging and taking her to see doctors, oncologists and radio-therapists, so I was needed on hand as her main carer and also English was not my parents' first language. My first and second line managers put their heads together, worked some IBM magic, and a few days later informed me I could take a month of paid leave, which was a huge burden off my mind. Unfortunately, my mother only survived 20 days from the day of her diagnosis, but IBM gave me a total of a month and a half off, so I had time following her passing to arrange the funeral, her financial and personal affairs, as well as prepare for the inquest into her death, the sale of the family house and care for my then 80-year-old father, who had become severely unwell around the same time with three fractures in his spine from osteoporosis, and had dropped to 41 kg in weight.

Since 2012, my father has had several other health-related issues and his vascular dementia has become increasingly worse. He is now 84, very frail, as deaf as a door knob, with a memory like a goldfish, but luckily content and comfortably settled in the house next door to me. I am responsible for taking him for visits to the GP, cardiologists, memory nurses, opticians, hearing aid specialists and dentists, ensuring he eats regular meals and takes his medication, taking out his rubbish, tidying up his house, doing all his administrative tasks, arranging social events with family and his friends and finding him when he gets lost. My brother helps over the weekends with cleaning and laundry.

I joke that I am in charge of all appointments for five people, including myself, and 80 finger and toe nails (luckily for me, my father currently takes care of his own).

Lately, I have noticed my father losing his sense of time, which I have been told is normal in a person with dementia. He gets up in the morning any time between 4 a.m. and 11 a.m., and he doesn't eat lunch or dinner unless prompted to do so. As a result, my work-from-home arrangement, which was originally a nice-to-have, has become more important, as I am able to make lunch for my father and take it next door during the day. It also means I am able to take a break at 15:15 hours on some days, run out to collect my two daughters from school which is fortunately 30 seconds' walk away from my doorstep, be back within 10 minutes and leave them downstairs with snacks and homework. I also avoid the stress of negotiating public transport or traffic back from an office in time to collect my two-year-old son from nursery at 18:00 hours. My husband works in a traditional City job and while he can drop off our son to nursery, he gets home late, after the rest of us have had dinner.

With people choosing to have children later in life and living longer into old age, this is a situation that is becoming more and more common: having responsibilities providing care for young children and elderly relatives. From a personal point of view IBM has given me the *flexibility* I need to support my family, not to mention the *compassionate leave* which allowed me to spend quality moments with my mother in her last days, whilst working on projects which I enjoy. In particular, my *work from home* arrangement which used to be a nice-to-have, has become more important as my family's needs have changed around me. The *trust and flexibility* that pervades the company allows a doctor's visit in my lunch break or a teacher meeting in the afternoon, with time made up in the evening (I am writing this at 22:49 hours on a Wednesday).

All of the above has the full support of the senior managers in my business unit. I have worked in different areas in IBM, including one with a strong presenteeism culture, partially driven by the client and lack of hot desks, where I was regularly leaving the house at 06:00 hours to arrive in the office at 07:00 hours to find half the department already present. This variation in culture has been a challenge when looking for new roles, and has played a part in decisions on career moves. I actually started a new job in IBM yesterday, and my main anxiety is not about the job itself, but whether my use of flexible working will cast me in a negative light. Flexibility is obviously not possible for all roles, but from my point of view a more consistent culture around trust and flexibility would make IBM even more family friendly[40].

## Employee Carer Needs at Different Stages of the Caring Journey

While working parents are easy for employers to spot, carers of parents, grandparents, partners or siblings come in all shapes and sizes and often feel uncomfortable

talking about their private lives at work. As a result it's
so important for employers to reach out, find out more
about their employees otherwise they risk losing their
very best talent.[41]

- When we first start to look after someone: and need
  time and flexibility to make alternative caring arrangements, as well as condition-specific guidance on likely
  progress of person cared for; advice on being personally resilient and looking after one's own health and
  well-being; advice and information; Carer Network
  for peer-to-peer support;

- When we first need to seek external help/advice from a
  health or other professional on behalf of the person
  being looked after: how to be recognised formally as
  carer; advice on Power of Attorney etc. to be able to
  deal with banks, utility companies, medical professionals; Emergency circumstances can result in an
  employee needing short periods of time off with little
  notice; this may require understanding and practical
  support from managers and colleagues;

- When you have to seek help at work: An increase in
  caring responsibilities may change an employee's personal circumstances and therefore they may need more
  flexibility or a change in work patterns, whether this is
  for a short while or for a long time, so need options
  for flexible working, leave possibilities;

- When you have to go part-time or give up work
  entirely: financial advice, for example, for future
  pension; keeping in touch and up-skilled during
  career break; option of freelance work;

— When paid care has to be introduced into the home of
  the person being cared for: professional help to source
  qualified care and funding options; and help with emergency care when usual care arrangements break down;

— If you move in with the person you are looking after,
  or they move into your home: your legal position, for
  example, to continue a tenancy if the person cared for
  is the tenant and dies; advice on managing the financial affairs of the person cared for;

— If you bring in live-in paid carers: professional help to
  source qualified care and identify how to finance; help
  with respite care;

— When the person you are caring for has to move in to
  a residential home: options for returning to work
  part-time or full-time; help with re-skilling and
  re-integrating at work; buddying schemes at work;

— End of life care: emergency and compassionate leave if
  still working;

— When the Caring Journey is over (either because the
  person cared for has recovered or they have died):
  coping with bereavement; work re-entry; getting
  co-workers and managers to re-frame how they see
  you. As Anne Richards, Chief Executive of M&G
  Investments and a leading gender diversity campaigner, says: 'A break of a year or two for a man or
  woman for caring responsibilities does not signal an
  end to ambition or a sudden decline in ability to
  contribute or lead'.[42] For some former carers, passing
  on their carer knowledge, for example, through their
  employer's Carers Network, can be an important part

of gaining closure and optimising the positive impact of their own learning.

## WHAT DO WORKING CARERS NEED?

Caregiving responsibilities, and certainly emergencies, occur throughout the day and have no respect for 9-5 work boundaries. And for many current jobs, work responsibilities themselves do not respect 9-5 boundaries, with emails, phone calls, etc. occurring at all hours. Families have no choice but to accommodate work demands into their lives. Similarly, whether employers like it or not, their employees must also accommodate life demands within their work schedules. For fundamental business reasons, such as workplace productivity and employee retention, employers must do more to help their employees with caregiving responsibilities to be more efficient and effective caregivers and to be less distracted by their care activities.

Some carers' needs may be very basic, such as leaving work on time or accessing a phone for personal use. Some may require flexible work arrangements on an ongoing, temporary or sporadic basis. It is important to consult a carer about which arrangements would be useful. These may include:

• A supportive culture that recognises and accommodates employees who have caring responsibilities

• Information for employees and managers about carer-friendly policies and entitlements under relevant legislation, awards or agreements

- Information for employees and managers about external assistance, such as carer support organisations
- Flexible work arrangements such as flexitime, part-time work, job-sharing, flexible rostering or compressed hours
- Leave provisions (paid family, parental, personal or carers' leave, bereavement leave, unpaid leave, flexible use of recreation leave or a leave donation scheme allowing staff to donate unused leave to carers)
- Working from home temporarily, sporadically or long-term
- A free or subsidised counselling service
- Facilities enabling carers to bring in the person they care for in emergencies
- Access to computers or phones for personal use[43].

As President Barack Obama's 2013 budget noted: 'Too many American workers must make the painful choice between the care of their families and the pay-check they desperately need'.

## HOW SUPPORT FOR CARING HAS EVOLVED AROUND THE WORLD

One of the leading international academic experts on caring and carers, Prof. Sue Yeandle, from the University of Sheffield, has described the evolution of institutional support for carers:

'Around the world, carers can aspire to access public policy outcomes of four main types. In the UK, elements of these were achieved, incrementally, and through political pressure, campaigning and evidence-gathering, in the following order.

First came *financial support* in the tax and social security system. This was a response to shocking revelations in the 1960s about the financial consequences for single women of caring, and to the argument that rewarding carers with poverty was grossly unfair and required the state to act to address a social injustice.

Next came *services for carers*, in the form of advice, information and emotional support; sitting, respite and breaks' services; and guidance and training on how best to manage caring. Historically, all UK carers' organisations have predominantly used fundraising, grants and charitable income to provide such services, although some have received modest local or central government grants. Since the 1990s, most local authorities have offered some carers' services too, often working with the voluntary sector.

Serious campaigning on *workplace support for carers* began in the 1980s, but it was only with the Employment Relations Act, 1999 that family members gained the right to take (unpaid) time off for 'family emergencies'. The Employment Act, 2002 gave carers of a disabled child under 19 the right to request flexible working (after 6 months' service), a right later extended to all employees in the Children and Families Act, 2014.

The fourth policy focus involves *recognition and rights* for carers. Arguably the bedrock of all other support, this is expressed, albeit weakly, in the Carers (Equal Opportunities) Act, 2004, and found a place in the 2008 *National Carers'*

*Strategy*. The Equality Act, 2010, responding to a European Court of Justice judgment, [7] gives carers some protection from discrimination in association with the support they give to a disabled person'.[44]

Sue concludes, however, that whilst the UK once led the world in carer campaigning, this is no longer the case:

'In other jurisdictions, developments in the crucial areas of carer rights, services and workplace rights are now moving ahead of arrangements in the UK. For example, Australia's and Canada's Human Rights Commissions are leading the way in emphasising what a human rights approach to care and caring can bring, in starting to articulate a right to care, and in setting out the frameworks needed to make caring a real choice for carers and those cared for – the only context in which good care can be assured. Japan, Germany, France, Belgium, Sweden and other countries are now using their long-term care insurance schemes and tax systems to stimulate the development of a wider range of care, household and personal services to ensure there is good support for care at home. In the best examples, these help carers to continue to provide the care they can manage and wish to give, without turning their lives and finances upside down or suffering the health or social consequences of caring alone and unsupported.

Increasingly other nations offer, or are enhancing, statutory paid care leave arrangements, something that is still completely missing in the UK, except in forward-looking companies offering voluntary schemes. Canada recently amended its Labour Code and extended its compassionate care leave to 28 weeks; it now enables workers to share this with another family member and to claim up to 55% of salary while taking leave, funding this through its employment insurance. In

Denmark, employers pay full wages during care leave, a cost substantially reimbursed through local taxation. Japan has recently amended the scheme it introduced in 1999 obliging employers to offer up to 93 days of family care leave, raising compensation to users to 65% of salary'.[45]

Caring for our carers: An international perspective on policy developments in the UK' by Sue Yeandle originally published in Juncture 23(1): 57–62. Published by Wiley and Sons Ltd for the Institute for Public Policy Research.'

*Reproduced with kind permission of Prof Yeandle, IPPR/ Juncture and Wiley & Sons Ltd*

## TAKE-AWAY

Most of us will be carers at some point in our lives. It may be for a short intense burst or long-term. Caring responsibilities may evolve slowly, or start suddenly after a major accident or a critical illness diagnosis. With aging populations, advances in medical technology and pressures on public welfare budgets, more of us can expect to be carers for longer. It is more likely, therefore, that caring will affect our work.

# CHAPTER 3

# CARE IN THE COMMUNITY AND THE WORKPLACE: THE BUSINESS CASE FOR ACTION BY EMPLOYERS AND SOCIETY

*Strategies, policies and practice to support carers, including working carers, are growing in popularity. Taking care of carers is also integral to a number of other workplace and public policy goals such as improving mental health and broader health and well-being; supporting gender equality; diversity and inclusion (both in society generally and specifically in workplace participation rates); engaging employees; creating great places to work; and restoring trust in business. Employers need to better understand the business case for their organisation to support working carers, using data which they capture about their employees to manage and improve their operations. Governments and societies too need to understand the irreplaceable value of the contribution of those caring voluntarily for a loved one.*

If it famously takes a village to raise a child, it equally takes community to sustain a carer. Unsustained, the cost of caring may be the failure to achieve a range of public policy goals such as gender equality, high rates of female participation in the labour force, fuller and longer working lives, social inclusion and a reduction in income inequalities and life chances. Unsurprisingly therefore, Robert Andersson of Eurofound and a former Chairman of Euro-carers, set greater support for working carers in the context of a number of European Union (EU) policy goals, when speaking at the Sixth International Carers Conference in Gothenburg, Sweden in September 2015.

Carers, Andersson argued, relate to five EU policy themes namely, the EU 2020 Employment Strategy; pensions and gender inequality; the 2013 Social Investment package for ageing and the costs of health-care; the 2014 long-term care and Social Protection strategy; and the 2015 Work-life Balance for families including a roadmap for work-life balance for carers.

As we saw in Chapter 1, a number of carer organisations and academic studies have attempted to calculate the replacement costs of unpaid caring.

It is not just that no government could afford these additional expenditures. No publicly provided paid care-services are likely to match the customised human touch of family and friends, no matter how compassionate, dedicated and experienced those individual paid care-workers may be. The sheer number of different clients that most paid care-workers have to look after, means they cannot hope to get to know in depth the individual life stories and interests of individual clients and to respond to these.

Just as there is a strong societal case for valuing, respecting and supporting family and friends who are looking after loved ones, so there are compelling arguments for individual employers to take care of their employees juggling work and caring.

Analyses of the pressures on public spending usually give prominence to the ballooning costs of health and social care budgets.

## WHY BUSINESS AND OTHER EMPLOYERS SHOULD CARE ABOUT WORKING CARERS

Although the scale of caring responsibilities presents a vast and growing social, political and economic challenge, it is in the interest of business and other employers to help address this challenge, particularly through the support of working carers they employ. Failure to do so impacts the resilience and productivity of organisations in a number of ways. The Positive Ageing Company (now part of Mercer) speaks of the 'Sleeping Tiger'. They define Sleeping Tiger as 'the negative financial impacts that your employee's family ageing issues are having on your bottom line, that you may have not yet realised or been able to quantify' (http://positiveageing.co/calculator/).

## LOST PRODUCTIVITY

Metlife estimates that American employers experience $33 billion in annual productivity losses by 23 million full-time employees who are also caregivers. Half ($17 billion) is attributable to the 7 million employees with intense caregiving responsibilities.[46]

Working caregivers in Canada report higher stress, increased absences and lateness as a result of their care work.[47] Other researchers have reported that caregivers may be less able to work overtime, travel for work, or take advantage of career-advancing opportunities such as professional development. They experienced more interruptions at work, lower productivity, and were frequently late or absent.[48]

The Canadian economy lost the equivalent of 157,000 full-time employees in 2012 because of caregiving pressures — a significant loss in productive capacity. According to the Conference Board of Canada, Canadian firms have been incurring about $1.3 billion in lost productivity per year as a result of caregivers missing full days or hours of work, or exiting the workplace altogether.[49]

## RECRUITMENT AND RETENTION COSTS

Some caregivers reduce their hours of work in order to accommodate their caregiving responsibilities. Research shows that the more time an individual spends caregiving, the less time he or she spends in the labour force.[50]

Canadian researcher Meredith Lilly argues: 'For both the employer and employee, being forced to quit a job in order to provide care is a most undesirable outcome. Employers lose the knowledge, skills and experience that the employee has developed over time, especially if the caregiver's decision to quit is sudden. The employer will also likely need to replace the departed worker. It is estimated that US business spends $2.8 billion every year to replace employees who leave their jobs to care'.[51] Lilly also quotes a UK study, suggesting it may cost the equivalent of 3-month's salary to replace a low-skilled worker, and more than a year's salary to replace a professional, who quits their job in order to care.[52]

## THE WIDENING SKILLS GAP

The McKinsey Global Institute predicts that by 2020 the world will face a 'skills gap' of nearly 40 million people, meaning that employers will need that many workers with a college degree or higher than the global labour force can supply. In their words, 'Businesses operating in this skills-scarce world must know how to find talent pools with the skills they need and to build strategies for hiring, retaining, and training the workers who will give them competitive advantage'.[53]

## LOSING OUT ON THE VALUE OF THE AGEING WORKFORCE

Look at any summary of global megatrends, and there will be reference to demographic change, the ageing of populations around the world, and therefore, the need to support older workers to be able to carry on working to a later age: fuller working lives. This is a theme of one of the Financial Times Business Book of the Year 2016 long list: The 100-Year Life: Living and Working in an Age of Longevity, by Lynda Gratton and Andrew Scott

(Bloomsbury 2016).[54] Since one of the significant reasons for older workers leaving the workforce, is to care for a loved one, it follows that helping working carers, will help keep older workers in work.

Employers around the world talk frequently of a global war for talent, even as some parts of the world, battling austerity, face parallel challenges of finding jobs for millions of un- or under-employed young people. Most societies are promoting greater gender equality and higher rates of female labour force participation but the ageing workforce also needs to be fully engaged.

As Business in the Community in the United Kingdom has noted: 'Older workers are vital for the future of the economy, and the need to develop a long-term strategic approach to recruiting and retaining older workers is crucially important for businesses. In particular, industries with a higher proportion of workers aged over 50 years will need to adapt their practices quickly to ensure they can retain and recruit the older workers who are fundamental to their workforce'.[55]

## RETAINING WORKING CARERS: AN EMPLOYEE ENGAGEMENT CHALLENGE

There is a compelling need for organisations large and small, in the private, public and third sectors, to attract, develop, retain and engage their talent. Hence, the explicit emphasis nowadays on health and well-being, mindfulness, mental health and managing workplace stress.

## Employee Engagement: Why It Matters to Business

All organisations, faced with the possibility of disruptive innovation and sudden, new, survival-threatening competitors coming seemingly out of nowhere, are constantly challenged to improve their productivity and rates of innovation. Promoting employee engagement has become an increasingly important priority for responsible organisations seeking to maintain their competitiveness in this turbulent environment. 'Employee engagement' can be defined as:

> *A multidimensional construct that comprises all of the different facets of the attitudes and behaviours of employees towards the organisation. The five dimensions of employee engagement are: employee satisfaction, employee identification, employee commitment, employee loyalty and employee performance.*[56]

Employee engagement has been associated with a variety of employee and organisational benefits.

For employees, greater engagement can:

- Enhance psychological well-being and a sense of personal accomplishment (Shuck & Reio, 2014);[57]

- Increase discretionary effort and reduce turnover and absenteeism (Kruse, 2015);[58]

For companies, employee engagement:

- Can promote higher profit growth (Kumar & Pansari, 2015);

- Promotes financial health and viability of firms, prompting researchers to conclude that boards have a duty to ensure that top management makes such engagement a priority (Lightle et al., 2015).[59]

## What Enhances Employee Engagement?

Given the importance of employee engagement to business value creation, employers and researchers have explored and identified a range of variables that can influence and increase it, both directly and indirectly via other factors.

- *High-performance HR practices* enhance job engagement as well as in-role performance. *Culture* can amplify this relationship, particularly if it is collectivist and power distance between colleagues is low (Lifeng et al., 2016).[60]

- *Relationships with superiors, job satisfaction and growth prospects, recognition and benefits, a good working environment and family friendliness* all drive employee engagement (Sivarethinamohan & Aranganathan, 2011).[61]

- *Perceived supervisor support* enhances *psychological empowerment*, leading to employee engagement.

- *Diversity practices*, moderated by *inclusion*, are associated with creating a *trusting climate*, which in turn is linked to employee engagement (Downey et al., 2015).[62]

- *Personal growth, recognition and trust* drive employee engagement (Kruse, 2015).

## How Support for Working Carers Promotes Engagement and Benefits Business

Support for working carers can be seen as part of a range of *'work-life balance'* initiatives designed to maintain employee engagement across independent spheres of work and personal life. However, a literature review by Benito-Osorio et al. (2014)[63] highlights the importance of recognising the connectedness of work and personal domains. A company — the domain of work for its employees — is increasingly perceived, not as a closed entity that competes with the domain of personal life but is instead an *'open system connected to its environment and is therefore involved in social, cultural, ethical and political changes'*. As a result, corporate social responsibility programmes which may have previously been externally focused now 'also include internal aspects, such as practices permitting work-life balance'.

> *As an open system, firms' performance is highly conditioned by stakeholders who have their own objectives. Indeed, firms' reputation is the result of an effective and committed relationship with its stakeholders and employees and their family are a type of group of interest. For this reason, work-life balance is a real challenge in the organisation that might improve human resource management and relationships with employees.*

This same review also found that work-life balance practices improve employee engagement, talent retention, productivity, costs and business results.

Employers for Carers in the UK argues that providing a supportive working environment:

— Attracts and retains staff

— Reduces stress

— Reduces recruitment and training costs

— Increases resilience and productivity

— Reduces sick leave

— Improves service delivery

— Produces cost savings

— Improves people management

— Increases staff morale.

A 2012 National Study of Employers by the Families and Work Institute and the Society for Human Resource Management (SHRM) supports this notion:

> 'Organisations that can offer more flexibility around reduced time, caregiving leaves and flex careers will have a **competitive edge in recruiting and retaining** employees as the aging workforce and dual focus on personal and professional lives among younger employees become increasingly important drivers in the labor market'. Being known as a flexible supportive work culture is not just good management, it makes good business sense.[64]

Specific family support interventions also produce business benefits, including employee engagement:

- *Training supervisors/line-managers to increase their family-supportive supervisor behaviours (FSSB)* can produce positive changes in employee job performance, organisational commitment, engagement, job satisfaction, and turnover intentions (Downey et al., 2015).[65]

- *Support for employees' children with special needs* increases employee engagement, productivity and retention, reduces corporate liability and enhances corporate reputation (Vogel, 2006).[66]

- *Supporting work-family balance*[67] correlates with organisational commitment, organisational citizenship behaviour, life satisfaction, job involvement and reduced intention to leave an organisation (Omran, 2016).[68]

- *Positive work-home interaction* enhances psychological meaningfulness and psychological availability and, in turn, employee engagement (Rothmann & Baumann, 2014).[69]

Complementing the idea that a company is not a closed system is the concept underpinning the work-family connection that an employee cannot be segmented into one entity for work and another for family life. Every employee plays multiple roles. Family financial and caregiver roles impact absenteeism and life satisfaction which, in turn, affects job performance. Organisations can develop family-friendly programmes and policies to support employees' multiple family roles (Boyar et al., 2016).[70] In addition, 'work-life balance' needs to be seen as more than just the juxtaposition of 'work' and 'family' but between 'work' and rest of life activities including dependent care and other personal concerns (Shankar & Bhavnagar, 2010).[71]

For work-family balance and other 'wellness' interventions to be effective, they must therefore *'move beyond the workplace and into the community; they need to be holistic health systems'* (Christ, 2016).[72]

## CORPORATE SOCIAL OPPORTUNITIES CREATED BY ENGAGING CARERS

The really lucky (and astute) organisations may find new market place insights from their proactive policies for carers. The installation of smart metres for electricity usage might be used to spot aberrations from the well-established routines of elderly people living alone, for example, the kettle always switched on before 9 a.m., between 2 p.m. and 3 p.m. for the afternoon cuppa, etc. This could alert family carers — often living a long way away — to potential difficulties, and thus provide extra reassurance to employee-carers. It could also become a commercial service as already in the UK.

'See home': A large company in the health sector raised the idea of partnering with tele-communication providers to put employees in direct contact with their home via a smart home-monitoring system. The company noted that knowing what is going on at home is a huge factor for caregivers and that this technology, by removing the element of surprise about the state of care, would be extremely valuable.

## TAKE-AWAY

Support for working carers makes financial sense but will be more effective when also linked to other societal and organisational goals and policies that can produce enhanced social, as well as fiscal, value.

# PART 2

---

# SEVEN STEPS TO BEING A GOOD EMPLOYER FOR WORKING CARERS

*Very great change starts from very small conversations, held among people who care.*

— *Margaret Wheatley*

# SEVEN STEPS TO BEING A GOOD EMPLOYER FOR WORKING CARERS

*As the stories in Part 1 illustrated, employers can support working carers to stay in the workforce and to return to work after the end of their caring journey. It is good practice to identify and consult employee carers on the design and delivery of policies and practises to help carers. Besides carer-proofing existing policies, specific initiatives to help carers typically include flexible and remote working, planned and emergency carer leave arrangements, advice and information, peer support and mentoring through carer networks, access to emergency professional care when usual care arrangements break down, technology-enabled help, especially for distance carers, line-manager training and a carer passport summarising previously agreed arrangements for the individual carer. These can be implemented through a Seven Step model for employers. Smaller organisations typically rely on more informal arrangements.*

In 2001, together with my good friend and colleague Adrian Hodges, I developed a Seven Step framework for companies wishing to manage Social, Environmental and Economic risks and opportunities. This was part of our book *Everybody's Business: Managing Risks & Opportunities in Today's Global Society.* Adrian and I subsequently refined our Seven Step framework in our second book *Corporate Social Opportunity: Making Corporate Social Responsibility Work for Your Business.*

## SEVEN STEPS

Step 1: Is about how a combination of changes in the external environment and heightened expectations from stakeholders cause triggers that impact an organisation. These triggers can stimulate revision of organisational strategies and operational practices.

Step 2: Scoping what matters is about identifying the material impacts that an organisation has.

Step 3: Making the business case is about how to build the justification for the proposed new organisational strategies, informed by organisational considerations and by overall organisational goals and business drivers.

Step 4: Committing to action is about the adoption of new strategy and the implications/links to organisational values, leadership, governance, organisational purpose and the value of making public commitments.

Step 5: Integration and implementation is about putting the new strategy into practice and embedding across the organisation.

Step 6: Engaging stakeholders involves engaging both internal and external stakeholders in implementation of the new strategy.

Step 7: Measuring and reporting is about collecting and disseminating data on the implementation of the new strategy and using this to trigger further progress and a further iteration of the seven steps for continuous improvement (Diagram 1).

**Diagram 1: Seven Steps Framework.**

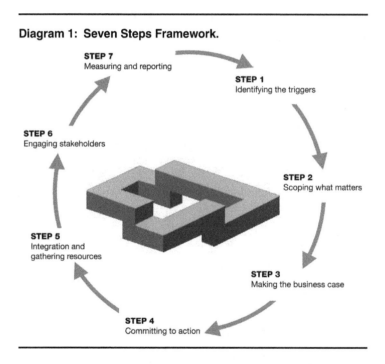

I think responsible employers could also use our Seven Step framework to help them to become a good employer of carers. Applying the Seven Step model to embed responsible business practices that Adrian Hodges and I developed to the cultivation of responsible business practices supporting carers, might look something like the following.

## STEP 1: IDENTIFYING THE TRIGGERS

The trigger for the employer to start to consider the needs of their employee carers, might be internal or external; top-down or bottom-up (**Diagram 2**). It could be an analysis of unscheduled absenteeism or employee departure statistics and exit interviews, showing a high number of avoidable resignations because of caring becoming seemingly incompatible with the day job. It might be an internal or external report, forecasting actual/projected skills shortages and concerns about loss of institutional memory as experienced workers leave. For some organisations, the trigger might be ideas tabled by employees or by trade unions as part of on-going collective bargaining. It could be a call from a professional body: The Chartered Institute of Personnel and Development (CIPD) is a professional association for human resource (HR) management professionals. CIPD is now calling on more businesses to adopt a formal policy to support workers,

**Diagram 2: Triggers Matrix.**

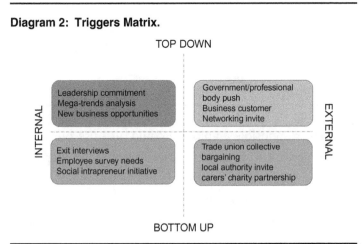

and ultimately benefit business. Dr. Jill Miller, CIPD Research Adviser, comments: 'Supporting those with caring responsibilities to balance their work and home lives, and therefore retaining our talent, is a key issue.[73] The trigger could be a C-suite initiative such as a corporate commitment to be a responsible business/responsible employer; and/or a reputational drive to be an employer of choice, a great place to work. For some, the trigger might be a presentation about and an invitation to join Employers for Carers (EFC) or in future one of the international equivalents that might start up. It might also be part of implementing new legislation — or anticipating future legislation'.

Katherine Wilson, the long-serving and highly knowledgeable Manager of EFC observes:

> *For some of the EFC members (e.g., in the financial services sector), it has been driven by employees with caring responsibilities/carers network leads, of varying levels of seniority within their organisations; while in other organisations [e.g., British Telecom (BT) and British Gas] it has been driven by a senior figure initiating and championing. For many, though, it's likely to have been driven by a combination of these factors — for example, support at BT and British Gas has been driven both by the economic and business case and by wanting to be a responsible business leader and — in terms of implementing and embedding this in the workplace — by an active staff carers network. Likewise support within Sainsbury's and PwC is likely to have been driven*

> *by a combination of senior figures championing*
> *this cause and a wider agenda about wanting to*
> *be a great place to work/responsible business*
> *leader.*[74]

In the case of social housing provider *Hyde Housing*, the trigger to act on working carers, was a combination of the then HR director having a particular interest in demographics and impacts on the workforce, coinciding with an invitation to attend an EFC networking event. She was enthused and persuaded Hyde to join EFC.

The trigger might be horizon-scanning future market trends or changes in the operating environment. For AbbVie Israel — part of the global pharmaceutical business AbbVie (which separated from Abbott Laboratories in 2013), the prompt to start thinking about employee carers, was a two-day management workshop with external stakeholders on megatrends. Data was presented on the growth of caregiving in Israel and the increasing number of employee carers. This prompted AbbVie Israel's Country Manager and HR director Sharon Graff to consult their senior management team (SMT). A show of hands revealed 40% were juggling work and caring — substantially higher than the national average of 25%. The SMT endorsed a move to survey the 100-strong workforce in Israel and consult them on how best the firm could support employee carers, through cooperation with 'CareGivers Israel' non-governmental organisation (NGO) and 'Eshel JDC'. Having completed the survey with the help of CareGivers Israel, AbbVie are working towards an action plan following the analysis of the survey results.[75]

## Exploring Business Purpose as a Trigger for Action

There is a growing interest in helping organisations to explore what is their fundamental purpose. *Blueprint for Better Business* — a UK charity — suggests deep articulation of organisational purpose has a number of purposes, viz:

- Inspire people to contribute personal energy to a collective venture.

- Reveal the human face of what the organisation is working to achieve.

- Ensure an authentic connection between what the organisation believes, what it says, what it means and what it does.

- Enable people to make practical choices about what they do day to day, using the purpose as a constant reference point.

- Enable people to have a legitimate voice where matters of purpose are concerned, both within and beyond the organisation.

- Reinforce the mutuality of dependence between business people and society — fostering the dignity and fulfilment of people and the flourishing of society.[76]

Redefining organisational purpose could itself be a trigger for examining how the organisation treats employee carers as part of the Blueprint framework: to be a responsible and responsive employer (**Diagram 3**). Purpose could be a powerful lens through which to scope current practice and employee needs (see Step 2). Helping an organisation

**Diagram 3: Blueprint for Better Business Framework.**

Five Principles of a Purpose Driven Business

**Honest and fair with customers & suppliers**

- Seeks to build lasting relationships with customers and suppliers
- Deals honestly with customers providing good and safe products and services
- Treats suppliers fairly, pays promptly what it owes and expects its suppliers to do the same
- Openly shares its knowledge to enable customers and suppliers to make better informed choices

**A responsible and responsive employer**

- Treats everyone with dignity and provides fair pay for all
- Enables and welcomes constructive dialogue about its behaviour in keeping true to its purpose
- Fosters innovation, leadership and personal accountability
- Protects and nurtures all who work for it to ensure people also learn, contribute and thrive

**A Good Citizen**

- Considers each person affected by its decisions as if they were a member of each decisionmakers own community
- Seeks and provides access to opportunities for less privileged people
- Makes a full and fair contribution to society by structuring its business and operations to promptly pay all taxes that are properly due

**Has a Purpose which delivers long-term sustainable performance**

- Operates true to a purpose that serves society, respects the dignity of people and so generates a fair return for responsible investors
- Enables and welcomes public scrutiny of the alignment between stated purpose and actual performance

**A guardian for future generations**

- Honours its duty to protect the natural world and conserve finite resources
- Contributes knowledge and experience to promote better regulation to the benefit of society as a whole rather than protecting self interest
- Invests in developing skills, knowledge and understanding in wider society to encourage informed citizenship

better live its purpose through helping employee carers could also become part of the business case for a carers policy (see Step 3). Explaining a carers policy as an integral part of a refreshed organisational purpose, could strengthen commitment to, and belief in, both organisational purpose and the carers policy (see further: Step 4 below).

Sometimes, the trigger for action can come from an individual employee as in the case of Emma Bould and Network Rail.

Emma Bould joined the UK's rail infrastructure operator *Network Rail*, as an entry-level information technology (IT) Programme Manager in 2012, after being sponsored through a Programme Management degree at Warwick University. Emma had been brought up by her grandparents, so when her grandma developed a form of dementia in 2010, it was natural for Emma to help her grandfather to look after his wife. Living with her grandparents, Emma would provide respite care so her grandfather could have some personal down-time at his golf-club or at the pub.

When Network Rail tried to set up a carers' network alongside networks for young mums, LGBT (lesbian, gay, bisexual or trans) and disabled employees, Emma went along — although up to that point, she had not thought of herself as a carer. 'My first Manager was pivotal in getting me to realise I was carer. He would ask what I had done that week end and when I always said nothing just looked after my Grandma, he would then send me links for different support. I think he knew I was very unhappy. When he saw this online about the carers network, he pushed me to go along to the meeting. He also encouraged me to house-sit when he was away on holiday so I had some respite time away from my Grandma and didn't have a long drive into work. I had a very unsupportive manager after him, but without him I don't know where I would be, he really did help me get the support I desperately needed'. She was the only carer to turn up.

'I don't like letting things drop, so I beavered away, putting up posters, sending posters to other Network Rail offices, creating an email group list and a SharePoint account'.

With the help of a secretary who was caring for a husband with depression, Emma effectively set up a carer befriending service within Network Rail. Despite her then manager being unsupportive, meaning she had to do Carer Network in her own time, Emma persisted.

Through googling and learning from organisations in Australia, Canada and The United States as well as in The United Kingdom, Emma gradually built up and populated a carers' portal covering the stages of the caring journey as well as information about major health conditions that people being cared for might have. She grew the number of Network Rail employee carers registered with the portal and MYRIAD (the carers' network) from 30 to 300. Many more people were e-mailing privately. It was not, Emma, realised an organisational culture where people felt comfortable about openly identifying themselves as carers: 'I don't want to be on a list of carers', 'I don't want my manager to know', were typical reactions. Overwhelmingly male, predominantly white and older, the Network Rail experienced high levels of health-related absences. Emma was eventually able to persuade Network Rail to join EFC based on a business case linked to reducing stress and sickness rates. MYRIAD went on to champion the development of a Carers policy for the organisation and continue to provide support to the thousands of carers working for Network Rail.

How an individual employee carer might take the initiative in their organisation:

— Check the organisation's intranet for any references to employees with caring responsibilities.

— Ask HR department if there is any support available for employee carers.

— Take advantage of any 'Town Hall' style meetings — either physically or virtually — with the CEO or Senior Management to raise awareness of the needs of employee-carers and to propose a carer's network.

— Volunteer to help devise a carer's strategy for the organisation.

— Propose a company webinar on being a working carer.

— Nominate Carer's UK (or equivalent caregiver's alliance in your own country) as charity of the year for your employer, to raise the profile of carers and caring and to raise funds for carers' charity.

— Introduce your HR Director to EFC (or any equivalent in your country).

— Keep a note handy of the URL of your local/national care-givers' organisation to pass onto colleagues when they talk about looking after a family member or friend.

— Share your experiences both positive and negative, of jug-gling work and caring.

— Volunteer to help establish an in-organisation carers network.

## STEP 2: SCOPING WHAT MATTERS

Employers then need to scope the most material issues affecting their working carers, without being intrusive, getting to know their staff and what their circumstances are. Which staff are employee carers? Can they be identified through existing, regular employee surveys? Are numbers close to national profile or skewed in some way? An older than average workforce is likely to have more working carers than the national average. The US coalition ReACT (Respect a Caregiver's time — see Part 3, Chapter 3, below page 219) recommends employers to: 'Add in a question during your employees' performance evaluations or one-on-one meetings that discusses their other responsibilities outside the office. Many times caregivers do not self-identify. By asking this question you are not only opening up avenues to help them, but you may also be helping them to see they are in fact a caregiver'.[77]

There are a number of ways that employers can learn which of their employees are also carers. Depending on the size and structure of their organisation this might be through the establishment of a 'carers register', or via staff induction, appraisals, employee surveys, etc.

Having a clear definition of what it means to be a 'carer' is important in whatever approach is taken — many people do not identify themselves as carers and may not think to raise the issue with their line manager in the first place. More commonly, people might describe their situation as 'looking after' or 'supporting' a family member.

## Standard Life

The insurer Standard Life is using promotion of a new Carer Leave scheme to encourage their working carers to identify themselves. Under the scheme, Standard Life employees who are carers, can have up to 5 days of paid-carer leave.

## The Scottish Courts and Tribunal Service Carers Register

The carers register is open to any member of staff on Scottish Court Service (SCS) terms and conditions who has significant caring responsibilities. That is, they look after a partner, child, relative or friend who cannot manage without help because they are physically or mentally ill, frail or disabled.

Carers who apply for the register have an appointment with a welfare officer from the Employee Assistance Programme (EAP), who assesses each individual's caring responsibilities before making a recommendation as to whether they should or should not be placed on the register. While staff are encouraged to discuss their application with their line manager, there is no requirement for individuals to disclose the nature of their caring responsibilities with their manager. Placement on the Carers Register provides entitlement to a range of supports and benefits (see further: Step 6 below).

### National Health Service Education Scotland — Workforce Online

At National Health Service (NHS) Education, Scotland, a new question was added to the existing online staff record system 'Workforce Online' to enable all employees to identify whether or not they are a carer. An organisation wide email, alerting them to this, and including a clear definition of what it means to be a carer was circulated, requesting employees to update their profile.[78]

Moving forward, data will be captured at the recruitment stage as all new members of staff will be required to populate their staff record. This includes permanent and fixed-term members of staff and part-time workers. The system is fully anonymous and remains open for staff to update at any time. It is not mandatory for staff to provide information which they do not wish/would rather not declare.

### Barriers to Self-identification as Carers

Some employees, of course, may be very reluctant to divulge their personal circumstances. They may fear it will have a negative impact on their careers; that, for example, they will no longer be considered for promotion. Canadian researcher Jacquie Eales from the University of Alberta, quotes one Canadian working carer: 'I really, really want to avoid anyone knowing' because of the fear of stigma and that she may subsequently be discriminated against, and no longer be considered for career advancement.[79]

As American caregiving expert and now Executive Director — Thought Leadership at Keck Medicine of USC (University of Southern California), Sherri Snelling writes: 'We are at the tipping point where more employees are more concerned about elder care than childcare', but 'a challenge for working caregivers and their employers is that caring for an older parent or ill spouse is not a joyful event. Workers don't show up with smiles and cute stories as they did when they were raising toddlers or had just become a grandparent'.[80]

Many employees, concerned about job security, fear identifying themselves as caregivers. A report by the National Alliance for Caregiving in The United States found 50% of working caregivers are reluctant to tell their supervisor about their caregiving responsibilities. In contrast, The 2014 Carer Survey conducted by Carers New South Wales, Australia found that the vast majority of working carers (84.7%) indicated that their employer knew about their caring responsibilities. Similarly, 76.7% reported feeling comfortable telling others in the workplace about their caring responsibilities, and 76.4% felt that their workplace supported them to combine work and care.[81]

Canadian academic Eales suggests that 'Self-identification early on is generally going to be preferable, before the individual has potentially reached that point where they are frustrating their line-manager or employer'.[82]

Not knowing about their workers' responsibilities creates a dilemma for employers. Some report caregiving resources and services available to employees go underutilized, causing HR departments to feel there is no need to keep them. In reality, there is a growing need. But both parties need to turn up the volume in communicating with each other. Men are more reticent than women to discuss their caregiving responsibilities at work.[83]

Employee surveys need to be conducted sensitively. Ideally, they should show the extent of the caring that employees are doing, and the costs to the business of the avoidable loss of talent when employee carers quit, with consequent productivity losses etc. What are the main challenges that these current and recent employee carers are facing? Employees in organisations which post many of their staff overseas to work, will have some very different challenges to those working in an organisation, located very close to where employees and their families live. What existing informal practices already exist to help? Which of these are effective and could easily be formalised?

The *Metropolitan Police Force*, covering Greater London wanted to encourage employees to declare if they were looking after someone. In order to help staff identify themselves as carers and to make them aware that the Met was starting work on carer issues, they circulated a leaflet with payslips and published an article in the Met's internal newsletter. A questionnaire was subsequently sent out about caring with the next set of payslips, with responses going to Carers UK so that employees knew their confidentiality was guaranteed. A report was produced by Carers UK from all the information gathered, which told the Met what the needs of their carers were. On the basis of this, the Met developed a carers' policy. The policy was publicly launched, with information and advice for referral to Carers UK posted on the Met intranet.[84]

Before deciding on what system of identification would be appropriate, employers might want to discuss with employees what they think could work most effectively, and what they would feel most comfortable with. This could be introduced with some general awareness raising, explaining why the organisation is wanting to gather information, and inviting employees with caring responsibilities to attend a discussion session or focus group.

## Johns Hopkins University, Baltimore, United States

The carer programme at the John Hopkins University, was developed by the Director of Work-Life Programmes and a committee that included the director of HR and the director of benefits, with the assistance of members of a caregiving taskforce. In addition, focus groups of employees were conducted to assess needs. Subsequently the LifeSpan Services Manager in the Office of Work, Life and Engagement became responsible for the operation of the carer policy.[85]

The reality is that identifying employees who are carers is not a one-off exercise. A combination of staff turnover and the reality that new carers are starting caring all the time, means that the exercise of finding new employee carers needs to be done at regular intervals. The good news is that becoming a workplace that is responsive to the needs of employee caregivers doesn't have to be complicated or expensive. It's likely that your organisation already has some programmes and options in place, and is applying some best practices in the areas of flexibility (agility) and technology.

Employers can use the list of 'what working carers need' (Part 1, Chapter 2, page 45) to begin scoping what their support for working carers might involve. A more sophisticated approach would be to scope potential working carer needs at each stage of the Caring Journey and how these might be addressed. (Part 1, Chapter 2).

## STEP 3: MAKING THE BUSINESS CASE

The business case should emerge from the scoping exercise, first in terms of direct cost-benefit analysis, even before taking into account more intangible and long-term benefits in employee engagement and advocacy, external reputation and potentially even marketplace insights.

My Carers UK board colleague, Ian Peters, recently retired as Managing Director of Residential Energy at British Gas, is clear about the business benefits of supporting employee carers. He says: 'I know that in British Gas, several years of having in place a well communicated carers' policy combined with a well-facilitated carers network hasn't just been about being a good employer, it's been good for business. We've seen reduced workplace stress and improved retention of experienced people, which in turn has led to higher customer satisfaction and lower recruitment costs'.[86] As a leader, Ian has been willing to speak out about his own experience as a working carer, looking after his elderly father.

Anne-Marie Slaughter is an international lawyer, foreign policy analyst, political scientist and public commentator. She was the Dean of Princeton University's Woodrow Wilson School of Public and International

Affairs, when then U.S. Secretary of State, Hillary Clinton tapped her to serve as the Director of Policy Planning for the U.S. State Department. Slaughter held this role from January 2009 until February 2011, when she very publicly stepped down. She has written that she came 'home not only because of Princeton's rules (after 2 years of leave, you lose your tenure), but also because of my desire to be with my family and my conclusion that juggling high-level government work with the needs of two teenage boys was not possible'. She subsequently wrote 'Why Women Still Can't Have it All' which appeared in the July/August 2012 issue of *The Atlantic* magazine. This quickly became the most downloaded article in the magazine's history and led to Slaughter's 2015 best-selling book: *Unfinished Business: Women Men Work Family*. Whilst principally focussed on the roles of men and women in childcare, Slaughter repeatedly emphasises in her book, that ageing populations make her arguments relevant to wider caring agendas. She advocates empowering men and women to re-envision their lives and embrace the roles of engaged fathers/mothers, sons/daughters and caregivers. I have been particularly influenced by 'Unfinished Business'. Slaughter's high profile and the very public decision not to extend her time at the State Department because of the needs of her teenage sons, meant her book generated international interest. In her book, she applies her formidable intellect to what will be increasingly pressing career issues for many more people because of the growing need for eldercare. In Take Care, I quote repeatedly and approvingly from Unfinished Business.

In terms of the business case, I fully identify with the arguments of Anne-Marie Slaughter when she writes in Unfinished Business:

> *How many articles have you read about the amazing benefits of exercise? Hundreds if not thousands have told us that just walking briskly for 30 minutes a day can regulate our weight, lower our blood pressure, reduce stress, boost our immune systems, and stimulate our brain. As journalists routinely write, if a single pill could do all that we would take it every morning. But somehow many of us find it hard to take the fairly small steps necessary, no pun intended to become more active.*
>
> *That's the way I feel about businesses that just don't get it when it comes to the benefits of allowing employees to fit together work and family. Reams of research demonstrate the impact on recruitment, retention, productivity, creativity and employee morale. Moreover, in an age of continual CEO laments about the war for top talent and of national worries about whether the American workforce is educated enough to be competitive in a digital and global economy, it's astounding that an enormous pool of highly educated and credential women in their 40's and 50's remain completely shut out of leadership-track positions because they chose at one point to ramp down in order to make time for care.*[87]

The insurer Aviva has revamped and improved its support for working carers and has chosen one of its largest offices — in Bristol in the south-west of England — as the site to pilot its enhanced support for carers. The pilot involved a high-profile launch onsite on Carers Rights Day 2016, featuring the CEO of Aviva UK and Ireland Life: Andy Briggs, the new HR director and a Customer Service Manager and local carer Adriano De Gennaro whose story is told in Part 1, Chapter 2 (page 28 above). I was delighted to chair the launch event, as chairman of Carers UK who are participating in the pilot through Employers for Carers, along with Mercer the world's largest HR consulting firm, and the responsible business coalition *Business in the Community*. The aim of this pilot is to test out whether as a result of high-profile support of carer support, there is a substantial take-up of the help available by Aviva employees who are carers and whether this has an appreciable, positive impact on rates of absenteeism, staff turnover and productivity, and, therefore, whether there is a positive return on investment (ROI). The Aviva Bristol pilot could be an important element in building the business case for better support for working carers.

What might be the business case that might need to be made in particular circumstances?

| Your Role | Your Possible Arguments |
| --- | --- |
| Individual, entrepreneurial working carer to his/her managers | Our organisational values include empowering. Helping those of us who are working carers is part of our organisational values and it is common-sense to support employees who might otherwise give up work to care. |

*(Continued)*

| Your Role | Your Possible Arguments |
| --- | --- |
| Carers network chairman to line manager | Supporting our carers helps make other HR policies like health and well-being, reducing workplace stress, improving mental health, increasing employee engagement more effective and better joined-up. |
| Head of Diversity and Inclusion to executive board | Caring for our workforce is now an integral part of diversity and inclusion, and being a responsible employer. |
| Executive board Carer champion to their peers on board | How many of us are looking after a parent or other elderly relative? With an ageing population, caring is becoming much more prevalent. More of our employees will be carers. We need to support them to stay resilient; and in the process help make our organisation more agile. |

## STEP 4: COMMITTING TO ACTION

Then the employer needs to commit to action. This may involve carer-proofing existing policies and publicising their relevance to carers; but it may also involve adoption of a specific Carers policy — or some combination. Whether an explicit or implicit set of policies for employee carers, these need to be consistent with corporate culture and circumstances. Ideally, the organisation will be able to explain these policies with reference to organisational purpose, values and how it defines its organisational responsibilities.

One company which has had a clear societal purpose for more than 70 years is the global pharmaceutical firm

Johnson and Johnson (J&J). The J&J Credo — first promulgated in 1943 — clearly sets out a logic and a hierarchy of stakeholder interests: https://www.jnj.com/about-jnj/jnj-credo. It is no surprise, therefore, that whilst it does not have a formal carers policy, J&J supports working carers as an integral part of aspiring to be a great employer. Prior to creating the programme, a group of employees met to discuss their needs and eldercare issues. This was an important source of information for designing the programme. Across the globe, J&J employees have options for part-time and flexible working and remote working. The global EAP (see Step 5 below page 122) includes help for carers. The J&J EAP in The United States has extra help for employees with eldercare responsibilities and/or caring for a disabled person.[88]

Carer policies will preferably be linked to overall HR and Talent policies and to corporate initiatives that build learning and good practice both for the company itself and for other employers, by collaborative initiatives through organisations such as EFC or one of the other networks for employers and work-life balance/diversity and inclusion, which are increasingly being contacted by employers about wider caring issues. It is important to note that studies show carers' perceptions of what is possible in their workplace may actually be a more important predictor of whether they remain employed at the onset of caring responsibilities than having access to formal provisions. This illustrates the importance of not just having flexible provisions, but of fostering a workplace culture in which employees feel comfortable using them. Simply put, organisational culture is 'the way we do things around here'. As management guru Peter Drucker famously opined 'Culture eats strategy for breakfast'.

A number of employers have developed a relatively short, specific carers policy, which makes clear the links to other HR policies and practices, which will be relevant to working carers. See EFC sample Carer policy.

---

### EFC Sample Carers Policy

_____You can replace _____ as appropriate to adapt this policy for your organisation.

_____ recognises that some people have caring responsibilities and that carers will constitute a part of its workforce. Carers provide unpaid care by looking after an ill, frail or disabled family member, friend or partner. _____ further recognises that employees may find it difficult to combine paid work and caring. We have, therefore adopted the following code of good practice in order to support employees who are or also who are likely to become carers.

This policy is fully supported by and integrated with other relevant policies such as:

Flexible Working Policy; Homeworking Guidelines; Leave Policy

This policy applies to all employees of _____

We reserve the right to amend this policy from time to time.

Staff will in no way be discriminated against on the grounds of their caring responsibilities. For further information, please refer to the Equal Opportunities Policy.

Employees are not obliged to disclose to their line manager that they are caring for someone but will be actively encouraged to do so. All line managers should ask whether staff they are supervising also have caring responsibilities, and should have due regard to issues of confidentiality concerning this information.

_____ welcomes comments and suggestions from all staff on how the organisation may further improve the working environment so that it is better equipped to deal with the varying needs of carers in the workforce.

All employees will be entitled to request time out in order to attend to the sudden needs of the individual that they care for. For further information, please refer to the Special Leave section of the Leave Policy.

All employees will be entitled to request to work flexibly (e.g., to request to work part-time, to work from home) in order to attend to the needs of the individual that they care for. For further information, please refer to the Flexible Working Policy.

All employees with caring responsibilities will be entitled to use the telephone at work in connection with their role as a carer. For further information, please refer to the Electronic Communications Policy.

_____ understands the difficulty that some carers face and is committed to providing as much support as is reasonably practicable. We invite the carers in our workforce to access and use the resources we make available to carers in the wider community, for example, advice and information, etc. Approved by

_____

Date _____.

## The Role of Leadership

A key part of committing to action is that the leaders of the organisation make clear their commitment and personally champion their organisation's commitment to working carers. As always, company leaders speaking out consistently on the topic is essential if employees are to believe the messages they are receiving. As EFC Chairman and ex-British Gas Managing Director Ian Peters says: 'CEO push is much more powerful than Human Resources pull!'[89]

It is even better if business leaders are willing to talk about their own caring roles — and best if some leaders were very publicly to take advantage of their own organisation's caring policies, to work part-time temporarily or even to take a short-term leave of absence. We know how walking the talk is a powerful example for others. (Although I can visualise market reactions and the feverish debate it would prompt among City analysts and business journalists about whether the business leader concerned was up to his or her job. And as a separate debate entirely, sadly one might also imagine differences in reaction depending on the gender of the chief executive concerned!)

When a business leader or senior politician is prepared to 'come out', however, we have seen the profound impact this can have on public opinion. Whilst sadly still not common place in all parts of the world, the example of top business leaders like Apple CEO Tim Cook and former BP boss John Browne who have spoken openly about their sexual orientation, has helped to encourage a younger generation to be more open and relaxed about their own sexual identity. More recently, the honesty of Lloyds Bank CEO António Horta Osório about his mental ill-health has started to challenge mental health taboos in the workplace, and encourage others to speak out too. We similarly need CEOs and other senior figures to talk about their caring responsibilities.

One leader who is passionate about setting a positive example and speaking out for other employee carers is Craig Hughes. After 20 years working for the international consulting firm EY, he joined PWC in 2012 as partner in charge of PWC's real estate practice.[90]

**Leaders Modelling and Speaking out for Employee Carers**

Craig Hughes and his wife Sarah have three young sons; 9 years, 7 years and 4 years old. The eldest (Rocha — pronounced rocker), is dyslexic and attends a special school. The 7 year old, Morgan, has cerebral palsy and autism but goes to an integrated school. Hughes is very public about his family circumstances and his caring role, and that he needs help. 'I know some people see it as a sign of weakness to ask for help. I don't!' he says.

He tries to be very public about working flexibly: 'My diary is open to anyone in the firm as are those of most of my colleagues. I am determined to be as fit as possible for as long as possible — so I diarise regular exercise. For one reason, I know that Morgan will need to be carried and sometimes constrained as he grows older and physically stronger'. Similarly, Hughes generally avoids early-morning meetings. 'I need to be at home until Morgan leaves the house. If I do leave before Morgan, the whole family has a lousy day. Only in extreme circumstances will I do an early morning meeting and then I leave before Morgan wakes up'. Craig acknowledges that it takes self-confidence to assert 'no meetings before 10 a.m.', but has found clients and co-workers to be very accommodating.

Hughes concedes that as a partner, it maybe easier for him to do this than more junior colleagues; but he strives to be a positive role model and to encourage others to take advantage of PWC's flexible working opportunities. He very deliberately seeks to hire into his team people who are looking for flexiwork.

'I feel I have enjoyed a successful career but this hasn't involved ignoring my family. I want to help create an enabling environment where carers can fulfil their caring responsibilities, have a successful career, enjoy work, have fun and feel they are making the most of themselves'.

The PWC has formal policies for flexible and part-time working and offers employees the option of career breaks (e.g., for travelling, study as well as for caring). PWC has also supported the creation of various employee networks; for parenting, disability, gender balance, LGBT, faith groups, and employees who are ex-military, as well as a carer's network. New employees are briefed on these networks when they join; and there are regular Network Fairs to encourage employees to get involved. Hughes sponsors the parenting network (set up about 5 years ago) and the carer's network, which began in 2011–2012.

When I first met Craig in autumn 2015, the PWC carer's network had around 100 employee members out of 18,000 UK employees. Assuming the UK average of 1:9 employee carers in the average workforce, this suggested 19 out of 20 PWC employee carers weren't yet in the network, although Hughes was quick to point out that employees didn't have to be members to access network services. Nevertheless, he was keen to have more employee carers coming forward. 'I am talking to Andrew Woodfield who runs our LGBT network. A few years ago, they faced disclosure barriers too. I want to see if we can learn from what the LGBT network did'. Taking advice both internally and externally, the parenting and caring networks were combined and re-launched in October 2016 as SPACE (Supporting Parents and Carers and Everyone else), also engaging likely future parents and carers. 1,200 staff had joined SPACE by the launch date, and 1,500 had signed up for the launch webinar.

Hughes is a highly articulate and credible role model, who is prepared to talk to clients and other organisations about working and caring. He is also an enthusiastic user of social media to get his message across, tweeting@craighughesPWC.

Another business leader who has not just spoken out but also written about his personal experience of combining work and caring is James Melville-Ross, a Senior Managing Director at FTI Consulting, a global business advisory firm, headquartered in Washington DC. James is based in London. He described his experience as a working carer in an article in International Business Times:

### James Melville-Ross

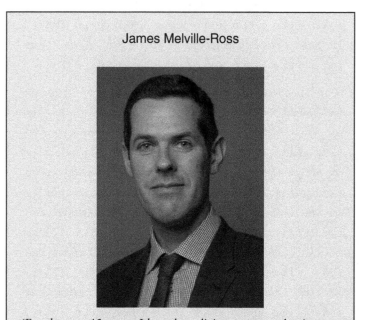

'For the past 12 years, I have been living an unusual existence. By day, I'm a City PR guy. At night, like some slightly rubbish superhero, I don my pinny and become an auxiliary nurse. My wife Georgie and I are proud parents to two exceptional, funny, engaging, loving and severely disabled twins: Thomas and Alice.

Our twins were born prematurely. They weren't messing about with a few weeks here or there, they were properly early — more than 4 months. We joked that it was because they were so keen to meet their parents, but we were laughing on the other side of our faces when the battle began.

Alice had four heart attacks on the first night of her life. The next day the South East of England suffered a power cut and the machines that were keeping our babies alive went down.

Then, on day 3, we were asked if we wanted to have Thomas baptised because he was going to die within the next 20 minutes. It was a rude and shocking beginning to our lives as mum and dad.

They made it, and after 9 months in hospital they came home, but the impact of those traumatic early days was that the twins would never walk or talk — they had severe quadriplegic, athetoid cerebral palsy.

It took us a long time to reconcile ourselves to the fact that life was going to be very different from thereon in. But slowly, we gained acceptance and eventually celebration of the miracle twins and the light they bring to the world. Their victories, so tiny for so-called 'normal' children, are their Mount Everest.

Like the time that Tommy and I ran in our local 10 k together with 1,000 other runners — me in my trainers, him in his wheelchair — and he slapped the bums of other runners as we overtook them.

Like the first time that Alice, through sheer tyranny of will, managed to say the words, 'I love you, Daddy' after 10 years of trying.

Like when Thomas got a powered wheelchair and realised that, for the first time in his life, he was able to go exactly where he wanted, rather than where we pushed him.

My second job starts when I get home from work. I help prepare medication for the night-time (20 syringes a night to be administered every hour), I give my son oxygen, I suction his throat if he has a cold and I run up and down stairs every time his oxygen monitor alarms. Then we're up every hour through the night, changing the twins, giving them medicine, turning them if they're uncomfortable and calming them if they go into spasms. At 5.30 a.m., my alarm sounds and the day begins again for job #1.

So does my work impact my ability to be a good dad? Or, looked at another way, how do my demands as a parent impact my ability to be half decent at my job?

I'd love to tell you that it's all been plain sailing, but that would be exaggerating. The second life impacts you in many ways. You feel torn between your work duties and the pressing needs of the family, and this leads to stress both at work and at home.

You worry if you are missing out on opportunities for new client work and promotion and that you have to cut back on travel opportunities. You end up using up holiday time for the never-ending schedule of hospital appointments. But I have been incredibly lucky to have an employer who has bent over backwards to accommodate my unusual situation.

At the start of year 1, I realised that I needed to be with the twins for 5 weeks of brain operations — my entire holiday allowance. Work said not to worry. Another time, Thomas was admitted into intensive care and nearly lost his life. Work said to take as much time as I needed. When my wife was on her knees with exhaustion after months in hospital with Thomas and I had to take 6 months unpaid leave to get the family back into shape, work didn't question it.

'I've been with my employer for 16 years. I'm sure there's a lesson in that. But my message to employers is to be understanding. You may find that if you are flexible, you develop a loyalty that cannot be found any other way. And also, that one day it might be you looking for some understanding'.

*Reproduced with the permission of James Melville-Ross and International Business Times.*

James Melville-Ross's book, Two for Joy, about his experience of being a father to his twins is published by John Blake Publishing and was released in June 2016.

FTI have now recognised that they need formal policies so that staff new to the organisation, less familiar with it or less senior/self-confident, know what help they can expect. FTI is developing a suite of diversity and inclusion policies under four broad pillars:

(1) gender;

(2) race;

(3) sexuality;

(4) mental health, disability and caring.

Tellingly James Melville-Ross observes that HR is putting support in place around mental health because 'it is now in the Zeitgeist'.

Despite his heavy workload and family commitments, James spoke recently at an FTI all-staff conference on the company's diversity and inclusion plans.

'You may be wondering', he began, 'why I as a male, white, middle-aged man, public-school educated and with a double-barrelled surname am speaking!'

James understands that many of his co-workers may not think of themselves as carers. He quotes one close colleague that he has worked for, for more than a decade. James knows the colleague has a serious caring responsibility for a close relative but has never seen or heard any indication that the colleague thinks of himself as a carer.

James plans to continue to talk about his own experience, in the hope that it will encourage other carers to identify themselves too.[91]

## The Importance of Corporate Champions

*Tim Fallowfield, Sainsbury Company Secretary and Carer Champion*

Tim Fallowfield joined J. Sainsbury PLC in 2001 as Company Secretary and joined the Board of Sainsbury's Supermarkets Ltd in 2004 as Company Secretary and Corporate Services Director. Tim began his career at the international law firm Clifford Chance for 6 years (1988–1994) and is a qualified solicitor.

Tim is a member of Sainsbury's Diversity and Inclusion Steering Group and is the Board Sponsor for Carers, Disability and Age. He is one of four Board Sponsors for Diversity and Inclusion. Other Sponsors cover: gender; race, religion and belief; and lesbian, gay, bisexual and transgender. They are supported by some 150 diversity champions across Sainsbury's. These champions promote all four pillars of Sainsbury's commitment to inclusion, although in practice, they will focus on whatever is most relevant in their part of the business. Having a dedicated board committee and champions reflects senior management's view that the inclusion agenda will gain greater momentum if it is clearly and demonstrably led from the top.

Tim Fallowfield is a regular speaker on caring issues both inside the company and externally at events to mark Carers' Rights Day and Carers' Week. He explains that: 'Our diversity and inclusion vision is to be "the most inclusive retailer where people love to work and shop". We will achieve this aspiration by recruiting, retaining and developing diverse and talented people and creating an inclusive environment where everyone can be the best they can be and where diverse views are listened to. This will enable us to anticipate and accommodate the needs of our diverse customers, reflecting the communities we serve'.

Tim's own experience when his mum was given just 6 months to live, 'confirmed to me what caring is all about. I had to balance my responsibilities to loved ones and commitments to my employers. At that difficult time, I received tremendous support and understanding from my colleagues, which really helped me to meet my caring and work roles'.

Sainsbury's are one of few FTSE 100 companies with an explicit carers policy and have worked with Carers UK for 15 years. For several years, they have promoted Carers Week, with many Sainsbury's stores across the country hosting events to raise awareness of local support and community groups. (Carers Week is an annual campaign to raise awareness of caring, highlight the challenges that carers face and recognise the contribution they make to families and communities throughout The United Kingdom. The campaign is brought to life by the individuals and organisations who come together to organise activities and events throughout The United Kingdom, drawing attention to just how important caring is. It is normally run in June each year. Australia also has an annual Carers Week.)

'Our commitment to carers grew stronger because of
our commitment on disability. Many carers are looking
after people with disabilities. Sainsbury's sponsorship of
the 2012 Paralympics made all this more important'.[92]

Another business leader in her time who spoke out
very publicly about combining work and caring is Dame
Steve Shirley. Her son Giles was autistic. She didn't just
talk about caring, but built a business that was designed
for people with caring responsibilities like herself. Dame
Steve's early experience of the 'glass ceiling' at work
encouraged her to set up her own IT software business
*Freelance Programmers,* in 1962 which, thanks to her
own family experience, she built up on the brilliant idea
of offering part-time employment to professional women
with dependants and perforce developed new techniques
to manage the business on this basis pioneering home-
working, job sharing and profit-sharing. The IT business,
later known as Xansa eventually employed over 8,500
people, was valued at $3 billion, and is now part of the
Sopra Steria Group.[93]

Making a public commitment to support employee-
carers, with a Carers' policy, seeking an external kite-
mark such as Carer Positive in Scotland (see Step 7
below page 152), and supporting carers' organisations,
reinforces the commitment to action. Management gurus
Collins and Porras famously coined the phrase *Big hairy
audacious goals (BHAGs)* to describe ambitious, stretch
targets that would galvanise an organisation.[94] Many
organisations nowadays have set sustainability BHAGs:
the global FMCG company Unilever, for example, has
the goal to double the size of the business whilst reducing their environmental footprint. What might be a

*BHAG* for employee carers, equivalent to environmental BHAGs such as Carbon or Water Neutrality; Zero Waste to land fill, etc.? Perhaps to halve the percentage or number of employees of the organisation having to give up work in order to care within a specified period — say 2 years? Or to achieve self-identification of employee carers within the organisation at a level consistent with the national average (or being able to explain why say a younger workforce means the organisation is showing a lower incidence of employee carers than the national average)?

## STEP 5: INTEGRATION AND IMPLEMENTATION

There are two aspects to how employers can help here — firstly, by enabling staff with caring responsibilities to manage their work responsibilities more easily and secondly by supporting them in their caring role. Integration and implementation of help for working carers will typically include some form of flexible, part-time working, options for tele-working/working from home, and enhanced leave arrangements (emergency leave, career breaks and/or specific Carer Leave). Typically, it will also include advice and information, access to experts to assess dependents and to help source/finance professional care services, and potentially access to free/subsidised support technology and emergency backup care. Some employers are improving implementation through line-management training and the adoption of 'Carer Passports'.

## Carer Passports

A Carer's Passport is for employees with specific caring responsibilities. It is a communication tool, enabling people to be supported at work. A Carer's Passport does not usually apply to childcare responsibilities unless the child has a long-term health condition or disability.

A Passport provides carers, and their line managers, with information about how the individual's responsibilities impact their work. It includes any solutions agreed between the carer and his or her line manager, for example, compressed hours.

A Carer's Passport will ideally stay with the employee should he or she be transferred within their organisation. It is available to any new line manager so they are aware of the employee's caring role and any solutions agreed. A Carer's Passport is not a legally binding document.

The entrepreneurial team at Business in the Community, Northern Ireland are promoting an Employee Passport as part of their Workplace 20:20 campaign for responsible workplace practices. The aim of the Employee Passport is to help make difficult conversations in the workplace easier to have and manage.

'The Employee Passport aims to give staff and managers confidence and provide clarity around personal circumstances that will ensure peoples' well-being', explains Tanya Kennedy, Workplace 20:20 Director. 'It helps employees and managers have open and honest conversations about individual circumstances — health, disability and/or caring responsibilities'.[95] The Business in the Community, Northern Ireland Employee Passport is based on the Carer Passport developed originally by BT — see below page 118.

## Access to Information

Having official carer policies is one thing but they have to be integrated into the organisation. Managers have to be trained on the spirit and letter of the new policies; the company needs to learn from experience; policies and examples of their implementation, along with access to internal and external resources, should be built into the company's intranet and knowledge systems. Employers will need to encourage all staff to be aware of and understand the organisation's policies on diversity and equal opportunities, including support for carers. This includes ensuring that all staffs have easy access to employee manuals, intranet, staff newsletters or any other information channels for employees as appropriate. As with employees taking extended maternity leave, it helps to find creative ways of keeping employees on long-term leave for caring, in touch and up-skilled so that re-entry to the firm, where possible and desired, is faster and more likely to succeed. This requires managers having a flexible mind-set, being prepared to 'think outside the box' and to compromise, and being approachable and consultative.

## Flexible Working

An increasing number of employers today offer flexible working arrangements for employees. This can be reduced summer hours or fewer shifts. Many employers also offer career breaks, for example, for younger employees who want to travel or pursue a sport or go to business school. It does not require huge ingenuity to adapt these facilities for working carers.

Working carers should be making common cause with other groups of employees who want flexible working arrangements: Those who want more time to pursue competitive sports (perhaps to aspire to the Olympics Team); to continue their education; to be involved in civic life, perhaps as a local councillor or a magistrate and so on; those who want to learn a foreign language; those who want to go travelling or to pursue a hobby more intensively.

FTI Consulting — the employers of James Melville-Ross (see above p. 96) promote flexible working for employees generally, which benefit working carers, including a set of principles to provide clarity regarding working from home, but which ultimately are based on 'trust'.

There is a wide range of options for flexible working and for leave specifically for carers, as summarised in the table here, from a report published by Carers Australia.[96]

### Examples of Leave Arrangements

| Policy/arrangement | Example of Care Situations |
| --- | --- |
| *Carers Emergency Leave*<br>For unforeseeable emergency incidents involving a dependent, when leave is needed for a short period of time. If more time needed, then absence usually becomes planned leave. | • To make longer term arrangements for a dependent's care.<br><br>• To cover when existing arrangements break down.<br><br>• To deal with an unexpected incident involving a dependent child at school. |
| *Carers' Planned Leave*<br>Leave needed for a foreseeable event lasting for a defined period. If more time is needed, absence usually | • Providing nursing care following hospital discharge. |

*(Continued)*

---

**Examples of Leave Arrangements**

---

| Policy/arrangement | Example of Care Situations |
|---|---|
| becomes a career break, or a review of working pattern/hours can be undertaken. | • Assisting a dependent to move accommodation. |
| | • Attending benefit/legal hearings with a dependent. |
| | • Attending hospital appointments with a dependent. |
| *Career Break or Sabbatical* | • Used when a carer has to take a longer period out of the workplace, but wishes to return to their former job. Not necessarily exclusive for carers. Minimum period usually 3 months to 2 years. |
| *Unpaid Leave* | • Usually used when all other paid leave options are exhausted. |
| | • Not necessarily exclusively for carers. |
| *Matched Leave* | • An additional period of leave offered by an employer to 'match' annual leave an employee has to take to provide care — often used to cover a period following hospital discharge. |
| *Compassionate Leave* | Used mostly following bereavement. |
| *Employer-covered Cost of Dependent Care* | To enable a carer to attend training, or perform work duties requested by the organisation — at a time when they would normally have caring responsibilities. |

*Source*: Work and Care: The Necessary Investment, Appendix 1: A list of flexible leave and working arrangements implemented by organisations in Australia and The United Kingdom.

# Combining Work and Care: The Business Case for Carer-Friendly Workplaces

---

**Examples of Flexible Working Arrangements**

---

| Policy/arrangement | Description |
|---|---|
| Flexi-time | Flexible starting and finishing times — adjusting the working day to begin and end earlier or later. |
| Home-working or Tele-working | Working in the home environment or other than in the normal workplace, often through the use of technology. |
| Annualised working hours | Completed contracted hours, but making adjustments to allow for shorter or longer days or weeks across the period of a year. |
| Job rotation | Moving from one job to another for a specific period to reduce work commitments during a period of care. |
| Term-time working | Working contracted hours but within school-term times. |
| Self-rostering | Team voluntarily agree shift patterns for managers to approve. |
| Job sharing | Two or more people fulfilling the requirements of a single post. Option of having a job share register within a company. |
| Split shifts | For example, arranged with a period of time in the middle of the day or afternoon. |
| Compressed working hours | Completing contracted hours in a shorter period than normal. For example, a 9-day fortnight. |
| Flexible combination | Ability to pick and choose, e.g., increasing/decreasing annual or unpaid leave for a particular working pattern. |
| Day extender | Working predominantly in the office but also carrying out additional work at home in the evening. |
| Phased retirement | Reducing hours progressively over a certain period rather than ceasing work completely. Often involves a cross-over period where the retiring employee helps to train their replacement. |

### Darren Fearnley, Chair of Carers' Network, Ministry of Justice

'I've been up all night with my mother'

After caring for his grandfather, both his parents and his mother-in-law, Darren is keen to tackle the stigma of caring. He wants carers to be able to speak openly about what it's like to be a carer, rather than feel embarrassed or worried about what colleagues will think.

Darren feels people more readily identify with the challenges new parents face than with the difficulties carers can experience. In addition, few people appreciate that being a carer can completely change the dynamics of a family, particularly when someone is caring for a parent and they find themselves being a primary carer and no longer a son or daughter.

The Ministry of Justice has strong flexible working policies, including part-time working, flexible working patterns and spells of 'emergency leave'. These can make the difference between a carer giving up their job or staying in the workplace, but there are still staff and managers who aren't clear about how these can be used to support carers.

Darren set up the Ministry of Justice carers' network 18 months ago and sends regular e-mail bulletins with information members may find helpful, such as the EAP. He has also helped design a carers information pack and developed intranet pages to help people navigate their way through the very complex system of support that's available to carers from Local Authorities, DWP and the voluntary sector. Carers UK and the Carers' Trust provide particularly useful advice.

> Darren and a small number of carers' champions in the
> Department promote awareness of carers issues — attending
> team meetings to get people thinking and talking about what
> caring means, and running stalls during Carers Week and on
> international carers' day.[97]

While other family-friendly policies facilitate paid time off at short notice, the carer's leave scheme of West Dunbartonshire local authority in Scotland, allows for an extended period of leave in order to care for a dependent. The scheme is unique in that it allows the employee to spread the cost of extended (unpaid) leave over a long period to minimise the financial impact of what is essentially a career break.

This scheme really demonstrates the council's commitment to retaining its employees with caring responsibilities, people whose only other option might be to leave employment. There is no break in service and employer pension contributions and other employee benefits such as annual leave and promotion opportunities are unaffected. The council benefits by retaining skills, knowledge and experience and improving staff well-being, resulting in improved engagement, loyalty and retention.[98]

The rapid ageing of the Japanese population, the mounting costs of eldercare, increasing numbers of women in the workforce, public debates about restricting the 'long-hours' work culture, growing interest in mental health and health and well-being in the workforce, questions of inter-generational equity are leading a number of Japanese companies to look at carer issues, especially eldercare — not least for distance carers.

One of the largest global food businesses, Ajinomoto Group offers 'Family Care Leave' – 'Absences or suspension of work can be taken to care for a spouse, parents, or family within the second-degree of kinship whom the employee supports. Leave can be taken up to 1 year'. Part-Time Family Care and Work Leave can be taken up to 2 hours and 30 minutes per day to provide care for certain family members until such care is no longer needed. Ajinomoto also allows Telecommuting. Take-up, however, so far has been minimal, suggesting there is still a shift in mind-sets required from both employers and employees. Perhaps as an early sign of such a shift, The Ajinomoto Group was in the national news Spring 2016 when its corporate unions asked for a reduction in working hours rather than wage increases.

In 2014, Mitsubishi Corporation (MC) launched the Diversity Office at Corporate Headquarters in order to support a diverse range of lifestyle needs, including employees caring for a loved one.[99]

## Family Care Support

This system allows employees who have family members with special needs to balance their responsibilities at home and at work. Mitsubishi has made improvements to better meet the needs of each employee, such as limiting overtime required, extending the staggered work hours and flextime system from a period of 1 year to as long as the care is necessary. A separate family care counselling service has been established to allow employees and their family members to quickly receive advice on a wide range of care-related issues.[100]

The Hyde Group, one of The United Kingdom's leading providers of affordable housing, referred to in Step 1 (page 72) have recognised the need to attract and retain carers in their workforce and the value of enabling them to stay at work. They have extended the option of requesting flexible working to all employees and also offer 'dependants leave' (5 days a year) and special/carers leave (5 days a year).[101]

Pharmaceutical company GlaxoSmithKline, which introduced its own compassionate care programme back in 2002, predating government legislation, offers eligible employees up to 13 weeks of leave over a 2-year period. Eligible employees with at least 3 years service receive 13 weeks pay at full salary. Since it was introduced, approximately 160 employees have taken advantage of the programme. HRs vice-president Tracy Lapointe says that while the programme demonstrates respect for employees, there is also a strong business case that helps with more practical goals like retention and staffing. 'Their colleagues know they will be away for a certain period of time, so we can plan for it as business, and have the right coverages in place'.[102]

In The United States, The Society for Human Resource Management's (SHRM) 2012 report, National Study of Employers Reveals Increased Workplace Flexibility – 77% of companies offer flextime and 63% offer telecommuting options for working caregivers.[103]

ThyssenKrupp, a German multinational corporation and one of the world's largest steel producers, has a life-phase-oriented HRs policy, called ProZukunft.

ThyssenKrupp offers its employees approximately 400 different working time models that are individually tailored to personal needs. ThyssenKrupp supports child caregivers through its onsite, company-owned childcare centre. It supports adult caregivers through a nursing hotline, in cooperation with Novitas BKK Krankenkasse, and, through company-owned services, advises employees on eldercare options.[104]

On the other side of the planet, Helen Johnson's employer (see Preface page xxvii). the financial institution Westpac Group was among the first Australian organisations to address issues pertaining to an older workforce (see box below).[105]

The Westpac Group is Australia's first and oldest company and bank. It continues to show its support for employees with caring responsibilities, comprising around 37% of its workforce. Building upon a long-standing commitment to employees with a wide range of responsibilities and interests, including those who are carers, in 2015 Westpac Group launched its 'All in Flex' approach. This allows its 40,000 people to choose how they work every day, making flexibility possible for everyone. A wide range of options include flexible work hours, mobile working, part-time work and job sharing. There are also a range of leave choices available such as carer's leave, parental leave, grandparental leave, purchased leave, career breaks and sporting leave.

'All in Flex' has seen new jobs advertisements clearly state that the role is open to an experienced candidate seeking both a rewarding career and flexible working. The rollout of 'All in Flex' included toolkits to increase people leader capability in leading teams who work flexibly. Employees are encouraged to talk through flexible work options with their people leader and team to come up with a solution that suits their role and which meets the needs of their customers. As a result of the success of 'All in Flex', uptake in flexible working across the Group has increased from 63% in 2014 to 74% in 2016.

To provide employees who are also carers with targeted support to succeed in their careers, Westpac Group expanded its support from parents to all employees with caring responsibilities. This includes those who are caregivers for children, people with a disability, their own parents or other family members. The Carers@Work Programme was built on the foundation of Westpac Group's Parents@Work Programme, which is provided and run through 'Parents at Work'. The programme consists of:

—  An information portal accessible to all employees. This provides a one-stop-shop for carers needing information on managing work and caring responsibilities, taking leave, returning to work, managing their careers and their well-being.

—  Four workshops, run monthly, include: Managing Your Career as a Working Parent or Carer; Preparing for Parental Leave and Staying in Touch; Returning to Work and Reconnecting; and Care and Well-being for You and Your Family.

—  Personalised one-to-one coaching aimed at senior leaders transitioning to and from parental leave, or during times of challenging caring situations.

Employee resources include the Westpac Group Carer's Concierge, a resource for employees who have older adult care responsibilities and an Eldercare Toolkit.

Otsuka Pharmaceuticals in Japan has a caregiver leave programme for employees: The Otsuka Group provides programmes to support employees with homecare responsibilities. For employees approaching the age of retirement, the Group offers work schedules tailored to fit each lifestyle along with opportunities for planning a fulfilling retirement life. Employees with family members that require care at home are encouraged to utilise the caregiver leave programme.

At Otsuka Pharmaceutical Factory, an employee questionnaire is conducted each year. Due to an increase in the number of comments concerning caregiver leave, the company decided to offer a seminar on the subject. The information provided includes the company's leave programme, the environment for homecare, and basic knowledge on the public long-term care insurance system.

Otsuka Group companies provide support to employees through an extended eligibility period for shorter working hours, flextime, half-day paid leave, and an accumulated paid leave system. There is also an I-Work programme for telecommuting. These programmes enable employees to realise their desired lifestyles and allow them to balance their work and family lives, even when life cycle events occur such as parenting and homecare.[106]

## SIGNPOSTING TO EXTERNAL SOURCES

If the opportunities for workplace support are limited, or if a carer needs support or information unrelated to their work situation, signposting to external sources of support, such as local carers centres or helplines may provide a route to valuable help and advice — this can be as simple as displaying leaflets/posters, etc., in prominent areas.

Euro-carers (the European Association Working for Carers) and INRCA (Instituto Nazionale Riposo e Cura Anziani) — the Italian think-tank: have developed an online portal as part of the INNOVAGE project to provide support to informal carers across the European Union (EU) who experience a substantial physical, psychological and financial burden.

InformCare — The EU Information Hub on Informal Care[107]

This includes information for employers in a number of countries including Bulgaria, Czech Republic, Germany, Lithuania, Malta, Poland, Portugal, Sweden, The United Kingdom (see Step 6).

---

Sainsbury's, where Tim Fallowfield (see above page 100) is carer champion, is the second largest chain of supermarkets in The United Kingdom, and employs 160,000 people. They want to be the most inclusive retailer, where people love to work and to shop. The company estimates that some 20,000 of its colleagues are providing care for an ill, frail or disabled family member or partner, friend or neighbour at any one time. The organisation is committed to supporting these colleagues as part of a wider recognition of the growing issue of balancing working and caring in today's society, and a belief in the role big businesses can play in driving progress and improving things for carers in the workplace.

Sainsbury's are long-standing steering group members of EFC and the organisation is proud of its leadership approach to supporting colleagues who are balancing work with caring responsibilities. The organisation is one of the few FTSE 100 companies with a specific policy for carers, which is known as the Carers People Policy, originally launched in 2011. The policy applies to all staff whether in stores, depots or store support centres. Staff say that a formal policy in place has made a huge difference in having conversations with other colleagues and their own line managers around the support that is available during challenging times, such as taking time off to go to appointments, changing schedules to fit around caring commitments or making adjustments to ways of working (e.g., allowing mobile phones on the shop floor in case of emergencies). Policies include flexible working, temporary or permanent changes to place of work, up to 4 days of unpaid carer leave each year, and a confidential, HR hotline.

Sainsbury's strive to create a positive workplace culture and encourage people to think about what it means to be a carer through involvement in campaigns such as Carers Week and Carers Rights Day. The organisation sees this not just as a support to colleagues, but also to the wider public. With over 1,300 supermarkets and convenience stores across the country, the organisation is able to reach out to customers and help spread awareness of local community organisations. Whilst it is up to local stores to decide whether to participate, the majority of supermarkets do join in, hosting local carer groups, meet-ups and information desks. Sainsbury's have had very positive feedback from customers about this direct involvement in helping to build more carer-friendly, local communities.

One of the very earliest corporate pioneers of taking care of employee carers was the UK-headquartered telecommunications company BT (formerly British Telecom). The sheer longevity of the BT commitment and the way that it has continued to evolve over time, in the light of experience, makes it a particularly important example.

---

## BT

The BT is one of the world's leading communications services companies, serving the needs of customers in The United Kingdom and across the world, providing fixed-line services, broadband, mobile and TV products and services as well as networked IT services.

The HR Director at the time, Caroline Waters OBE explains, 'Part of my role as HR director was horizon-scanning — looking at the HR implications of demographic change, economic and social trends, potential future legislation and so on. Back in 1997, I could see the population was ageing and that caring was going to become a big issue'.

One of the first things BT did was to form a partnership with Carers UK in 1999.

As a member of the current D&I team observes, 'this was fundamental to the success of our approach. Carers UK shared with us their expertise and worked with us to create a framework of simple flexibility and practical support that our carers needed to manage their professional and caring responsibilities in harmony'.

The BT's first Carers' Policy was launched in 1999. Part of the challenge was that there were no visible role models to learn from. BT ran a couple of events for carers but hardly anyone turned up. Employees at that time simply did not identify themselves as 'carers'.

In 2000, BT started using its intranet to reach out to those employees who were carers and begin a conversation. BT carers

commented it would be easier to juggle work and caring responsibilities if they had a line manager who was aware of their situation and by using their right to urgent leave to cover
emergencies in their caring role. Crucially, at the same time,
senior leadership recognised this was a growing challenge for
BT's carers; they supported the internal debate about how to
support the business needs and their employees carers needs at
the same time.

## British Telecom Carers Passport

The BT worked with small groups of carers to understand what
they needed. One of the major pieces of feedback was people
were finding it difficult to start a conversation with their manager about their caring responsibilities. So, BT created the
Carers Passport. This is a simple word document that can be
downloaded from the intranet, by anyone at BT who believes
their caring responsibilities could have an impact on their ability
to work currently or at sometime in the future. The Passport
gives the individual the opportunity to describe their caring
responsibilities, any adjustments they might need and an agreement between the individual and their line manager if they need
to leave work suddenly or are not able to come into work. It's
called a Passport because if the individual moves roles, then
they take the document with them, to start a new conversation
with their new manager. Equally, if their manager moves on to
another role, the document is shared with the new manager,
who is quickly bought up to speed with the individual's caring
responsibilities and requirements.

Importantly, the passport reduced the need to start potentially difficult conversations with a new line manager before the working

carer knew them or felt comfortable confiding in them. Another goal of the Carers Passport was to stop employees feeling that because of their caring responsibilities, their career would stall.

The Carers Passport and the Carers Policy were promoted widely on the BT intranet and helped generate awareness and a language to talk about employee carers. Individuals started to self-identity and share tips and experiences — as did line managers of employee carers. Ex-carers were especially enthusiastic and keen to mentor current carers.

## Being Prepared to Care

The BT worked hard to help the rest of the workforce understand what it was like to be a carer, how caring responsibilities could start suddenly, what support there was in BT and further afield for them. They put all this information into a booklet called 'Helping You Care' which was aimed at people who didn't have any caring responsibilities at the moment but could do in an instant.

The company appointed a carers champion from BT's senior management team; someone who had first-hand experience of being a carer and was ready to share that experience across BT. Initially, this was Sally Davis — then CEO for the BT Wholesale business and herself a highly visible carer for a very elderly mum. Davis was a real-life example of an employee carer who had negotiated her own flexible working arrangement with her line manager — in her case the CEO! Davis importantly was willing to speak out about her own carer experience. By then, BT knew that having a senior-level champion for carers was essential and when Davis left the business, she was replaced by another senior-level champion.

## Carers Network

All this work led to the establishment of the BT Carers Network in 2010. BT has seven people networks, including Able2 (disability), Gender Equality, Ethnic Diversity, LGBT+, Christian and Muslim. The aim of the Carers Network is to provide a single focal point for carers in the company; to build a strong mutual support network building on the collective knowledge and insights of BT's carers; to provide links to external networks with specialist knowledge about caring for people with particular conditions. The network is also a source of role models and case studies of other carers across the business and how they had juggled their caring and work responsibilities successfully. Today the Carers network continues to hold regular knowledge calls — and the recordings of these are uploaded onto the Carers intranet site for those people who can't listen in real time — on a range of subjects, bringing in external experts to bring the latest thinking and answer questions from our carers and those people who manage carers. The network is now the third biggest of the seven BT people networks.

Inevitably, in a large multinational company like BT, at the outset, almost 20 years ago now, implementing a new policy to support carers was not without challenge. At the time, the role of the carer wasn't discussed openly and very few people realised how many BT people were juggling caring responsibilities with their day job. But, as BT realised, modern life and especially business life is more demanding; people are more geographically mobile, families are more complex and diverse, and traditional caring patterns have often broken down.

Importantly, today after almost 20 years practical experience as an employer of carers, BT has embedded caring as an integral part of its overall Inclusion Policy. The Carers Passport too is now part of a broader employee passport scheme, as the learning and advantages of tailored support for working carers has been transferred to other contexts.

As Candice Cross, the current Group Head of Diversity and Inclusion says:

'We passionately believe that supporting carers in our organisation isn't difficult, disruptive or expensive. It's just plain business sense. Whether it's a small change in working hours or flexible arrangements — these can make all the difference to both the carer and our business'.

## Making Full Use of Employee Assistance Programmes

Employers can offer carers the access to health and well-being support initiatives or EAPs if these are available through the workplace; and be very explicit that carers are eligible for this help.

The EAPs are employee benefit programmes offered by many employers. EAP are intended to help employees deal with personal problems that might adversely impact their work performance, health and well-being. EAP generally include assessment, short-term counselling and referral services for employees and their immediate family.

The EAPs typically include support for employees on a wide range of issues, including work, health, debt, emotional, personal, family and legal. Free telephone support is typically available 24 hours a day all year round, with additional online and face-to-face counselling also often part of an EAP package. EAP assistance can provide access to health and well-being programmes, stress management, healthy eating and weight management as well as general information and advice on a range of issues. EAP may offer a variety of resources for caregivers including educational information, planning tools, geriatric experts able to help find a suitable carehome or live-in carer, and referrals to other helpful organisations. Some leading (larger) employers also offer practical support such as care search and backup care and eldercare services through EAPs. However, this is still relatively rare compared with childcare.

The 3M's EAP, for example, can assist their employees in finding:

Transportation services

Home health-care

Geriatric care management

Adult day-care

Meal programmes

Rehabilitation centres

Medicare/Medicaid information

Independent and assisted living options

Nursing homes

Emergency response procedures.

The EAP also offers help with long-distance caregiving issues, respite services, community resources, support groups and referrals are also available.[108]

Harvard University's EAP offers immediate, free, confidential help for all Harvard employees and their household members. The EAP provides advice and recommendations on any elder- or adult-care issue, and referrals to resources nationwide. The Senior Care Planning programme helps faculty and staff navigate the ever-changing demands of caring for an aging family member or other adult by connecting them with a professional senior care advisor, a licensed geriatric social worker who is an expert in adult- and eldercare. The programme also provides referrals and access to vetted services around the country. This includes backup care if an adult relative's needs or care arrangements suddenly change or their regular care is unavailable, the Harvard EAP can find backup care to cope with a short-term need.[109]

Significantly, Mercer has recently acquired Positive Ageing Co which helps organisations, employees and families to prepare for and manage ageing, eldercare and later life.

## Access to Emergency Backup Care

Some employers are also providing backup for employees when their usual paid-care arrangements break down. In practice, this is proving harder to provide for eldercare (where needs are more complex and individual) than typically for childcare.

Unilever — the multinational FMCG company has a Family-Friendly benefits — Backup Care: For adult/elderly dependents and children when care arrangements break down, or if you or any member of your family need temporary support as a result of illness, injury or surgery (Diagram 4).[110]

Deloitte Ireland's Emergency Backup Dependent care. This service can be used when employees need to be at work and their regular child or adult/eldercare is unavailable. Care is available for infants through teenage children and adult relatives of Deloitte employees, up to a maximum of 30 days per employee per fiscal year.

## Access to Specialist Expertise on Care Options

Astellas, the Japanese-headquartered pharmaceutical company, offers a range of benefits such as use of a professional geriatric care manager to meet with a dependent elder of an employee, to assess needs, create a care plan and walk the caregiver through options for community services and other help.[111]

Emory University in The United States runs caregiver workshops and access to a professional geriatric care manager network. These have high utilisation rates among Emory's caregiving faculty and staff. The growing demand for caregiver guidance recently led the school to add an Onsite Care Consultant.

Taisei Corporation, which is one of the biggest construction companies in Japan, is famous for advanced measures on supporting employees' combining work and elderly care.[112]

**Diagram 4: Unilever Employee Poster.**

## CARING FOR A DEPENDANT?

**If you have a caring responsibility, we have policies and resources to support you, including:**

### EMPLOYEE ASSISTANCE PROGRAMME

There's a wealth of information on the sections of Workplace Options about planning for the future, supporting adults with disabilities, becoming a carer and coping with grief and loss.

### UNPAID LEAVE

You may be eligible for a one-off block of time away from work which is above and beyond your holiday entitlement.

### BACK-UP CARE

Arrange for an in-home care worker to support your family member with their care needs.

FOR MORE INFO VISIT
INSIDE.UNILEVER.COM
Services > MY HR SERVICES
or speak to your **local HR
ADVISOR** for more details.

SUPPORTING U

Policies and Practical Support for Everyone

*Source*: Reproduced with permission of Unilever plc.

The Federal National Mortgage Association in The United States, commonly known as Fannie Mae is a government-sponsored enterprise and, since 1968, a publicly traded company. Its aim is to expand the secondary mortgage market by securitising mortgages. Fannie Mae's eldercare programme began in 1999 and includes Eldercare consultations (in-person or remote). The consultation service can be used for any care situation facing the employee, including care for in-laws and grandparents. Consultations can also include conference calls with siblings and joint consultations with spouses. The consultation service is unique in that it relies upon a geriatric care manager/licensed clinical social worker that is housed at Fannie Mae, but is employed by Iona Senior Services, a non-profit service agency. The social worker oversees the programme and provides consultations directly.[113]

## Line Managers

Much depends on the attitudes and behaviours of line managers. As Anne-Marie Slaughter writes in Unfinished Business:

> *To be stigmatized means to be singled out, shamed and discriminated against for some trait or failing. Stigma based on race, creed, gender, or sexual orientation is sharply and explicitly disapproved of in contemporary American Society. Why should stigma based on taking advantage of company policy to care for a loved one be any different? Workers who work from home or even take time off do not lose IQ points. Their choice to put family alongside or even ahead of career advancement does not necessarily affect the quality of their work, even if it reduces the quantity. (Anne-Marie Slaughter, Unfinished Business, p. 63)*

Line managers are increasingly seen as the key to unlocking the full potential of flexible working, but to do this they need support and training to develop skills around managing different working patterns, and building trust with their teams. In this context, line-manager training around flexibility is moving away from an opt-in option, to a required competence. Getting line managers to see the benefits of flexibility is, as these case studies demonstrate, easier when it is clear how it aligns with the overall strategy and plan, and people understand the 'why'. Several employers with established care policies report that initial resistance tended to be strongest lower down the management chain where arguably life is simpler, but also tougher with tight targets, etc. — so for line managers, a carers' policy can be yet another thing to have to learn about and to take into consideration. Some employers have also found that there was a psychological challenge in dealing with returning, ex-carers, for some line managers: 'this person hasn't been/seemed interested for the last few years, in developing their careers. Now they are again. As their line manager, I have to rethink how I view them!' In practice, this was a similar situation to those returning from maternity leave or a long-term leave due to physical or mental illness.

One company that has placed great emphasis on line-manager training is the Unipart Group which is a multinational manufacturing, logistics and consultancy company headquartered in Cowley, Oxfordshire, England. Unipart for more than a quarter of a century has emphasised long-term, shared destiny relationships with all its stakeholders — particularly employees. The Unipart Way is a corpus of knowledge and organisational philosophy emphasising the inclusive company and long-term value creation. In line with The Unipart Way, the organisation aims to understand the needs of individual employees, recognising that these will change over time and on finding individual solutions rather than one size fits all approaches.

'Managing pressure The Unipart Way' is a line-manager training programme. Part of the course aims to alert managers to stress symptoms that they might see in staff, explicitly including arising from being a carer. The course trains managers to initiate conversations with their colleagues, including exploring what might be the causes of stress. There is not a formal company-wide carer's policy, but Unipart has a Flexible Working Policy through which line managers are encouraged to work with individual staff to find appropriate accommodations.

In practice, part-time working or leave is often the last thing that staff want, because in many cases, they are finding solace at work. What Unipart finds works better, is showing understanding of the individual's position, allowing them the flexibility to leave a bit earlier, take a few hours off work, or to work from home — which is not disruptive and allows people still to do their job.

Frank Nigriello, Unipart's Director of Corporate Affairs, explains: 'We require a great deal of creativity and innovative thinking from our employees, so employee engagement is fundamental to The Unipart Way. When things happen in people's lives, we want to help them in a way that keeps them engaged and committed, while enabling them to continue to contribute to the team. People who need greater flexibility in their working patterns do not want to feel that they are letting their colleagues down or that they are not doing their job because they are reducing their hours to care for a relative'.

'We are training our managers and team leaders to be sensitive to these situations and to find practical solutions that work for both the employee and the company. We take this extremely seriously. Wherever possible, we try to balance an individual's needs with our need to consistently meet the real and perceived needs of our customers. That is a key role of line management'.[114]

The Unipart Group won the Well-being at Work award in the 2016 responsible business awards, administered by the charity Business in the Community in the United Kingdom.

Also in the United Kingdom, the Open University E-learning resource for line managers 'Caring Counts in the Workplace' is an online course (also freely accessible externally) to help managers and staff develop a clearer understanding of the issues faced by carers as they juggle their caring role with their working life. As Rupert McNeil, Chief People Officer, of the UK Civil Service notes, caring 'is often a very difficult and emotionally challenging. A considerate line manager can make all the difference to some of our most caring people, giving them the flexibility and opportunities they need to thrive'.[115]

### Line-Manager Training Strategy: Practical Tips from Disability Campaigning

Susan Scott-Parker, OBE is internationally recognised as a spirited and creative thought leader on how to mobilise business behind the economic and social inclusion of people with disabilities worldwide. She has made a long-term commitment to challenging outdated assumptions regarding both disability as it affects business and the potential of responsible business to adapt respectfully for human reality.

Susan pioneered the first business disability network, working to the mutual benefit of business and disabled people. This was launched in 1991 by HRH, The Prince of Wales as Employers Forum on Disability, now Business Disability Forum. Susan ran EFD/BDF for a quarter century, before moving at the end of 2015, to run Business Disability International, which she also created. This seeks to mobilise the collective power of global businesses to liberate the potential of disabled people worldwide.

Susan and I worked closely together when I chaired the UK's National Disability Council in the 1990s; and I have long admired her energy, focus and passionate commitment.

I challenged Susan to extrapolate from her long experience working with employers on disability issues, to identify key lessons for successful line-manager training on work and caring. She was typically forthright in her response.

'The ideal would be to infiltrate existing courses — instead of a special course on disability or carers, we want the performance management course for managers to simply also ask: what should you do when someone's performance is affected by their caring responsibilities or their/disability, etc.? Ditto for other existing line-manager training such as sickness absence management, stress

management, managing for resilience, promoting well-
being.

Our message is always to minimise special one offs —
though some will be needed — but they work best when
designed to make it easier to articulate the need to change
and to feel personally comfortable when discussing the
need for change. That is why I would suggest training
that doesn't feel like training is best targeted at the senior
executive level. Training for managers should probably
be focused on spelling out what they have permission to
do and how they will be rewarded and spelling out
behaviour which will not be tolerated, while building
core competencies to encompass these particular areas'.

Susan is clear that employers need 'to do an old fash-
ioned training needs analysis — what should managers
know and do versus what do they actually know and do?
And only then ask: how might training fit with our
Organisational Development (OD) strategy?'

Employers, she says, need to define a strategic change
or OD model – 'how do we best change our people's
worldview and behaviour? — how do we articulate the
rationale for change and describe our destination? How
do we reward people who get it right — how do we
make it clear what we will not tolerate? How do we provide the resources needed to promote the change?'

Susan is clear, however, that employers need first to
audit policies, procedures, culture to ensure that they are
fit for purpose; and consistent with what line managers
are being asked to do. Beware situations where 'trainers
ask manager attendees to behave in ways contra-indicated
by company policy such as: 'you must make adjustments
when someone becomes disabled or a carer .... but

attendees all know that the sickness policy remains the same and HR refuse to change it so in fact, the line managers cannot make the adjustment required. The classic for carers will be the training that says the manager should be flexible — and the policy which punishes the manager who doesn't hit his targets'.

Beware too the training 'done by trainers reading a PPT deck — with no personal experience who invoice as experts but are not ... and who put the political correctness fear of God into the poor participants!'

By contrast, argues Susan Scott-Parker, what works is where "the training is part of a structured OD strategy which is informed by journey analyses; 'what barriers in the company's control get in the way — when a person moves through the employment journey?'

The training is only done after the company removes the obstacles actually caused by the company, and after it has identified those which are truly caused by the line managers — and so everyone is clear: 'What do line managers need to do differently?' and 'what should the company do differently which is most likely to make it easier for them to change'". Susan says The Lloyds Bank Group policy is exemplary in that they give explicit permission to their managers to tolerate a 10% drop in productivity when someone going through a bad patch.[116]

Negative attitudes in the workplace can lead carers to avoid discussing their caring roles, and to shy away from seeking formal support. It was striking that even those carers who had discussed their caring roles with their employer described having had to be 'brave' or 'assertive' to do so. This meant a 'changed identity'.

The charities Age UK and Carers UK have, therefore, suggested employers could create a single point of contact for carers within the workplace — akin to a union representative, or even a 'Care Aider' (like a First Aider). The aim of these schemes would be to offer carers an approachable third party with whom they could discuss any challenges they were facing, and who could support them in discussions with line managers.[117]

## STEP 6: ENGAGING STAKEHOLDERS

As with any other aspects of responsible business practices, the wise company engages stakeholders and builds partnerships — in this instance, encouraging staff with caring responsibilities to set up their own support group or join an existing network if the company has one. Employers have an obvious need to engage both employee carers and other employees who may be negatively impacted by extra work or sudden need to cover for employee carers, etc. Good communication of carer policies and procedures is essential to getting this right. This can be achieved on a number of levels, from the provision of basic information via staff induction processes, payslip messages, organisation intranet, staff message boards, etc., to wider workplace awareness raising sessions involving colleagues and managers (**Diagram 5**).

### Wheatley Group 'People like Me' Portal

The People Like Me portal was developed in May 2014 by the Scottish social housing provider The Wheatley

**Diagram 5: London Fire Brigade Carers Portal.**

Group. This was launched by carrying out roadshows at 52 local offices to raise awareness of the content and support it provides, it is promoted and signposted in e-mails, blogs, staff newsletters and any visits to local offices/teams. The portal has a dedicated Carers page and is regularly updated with information and dates of carers' support group meetings to actively encourage carers to participate. Wheatley is able to access monthly statistics for hits on the Carers page, to check that this resource is being used. Wheatly also has a senior-level Ambassador for the carers support group, helping to promote the work to support carers throughout the business and to raise awareness of the issues that working carers face.[118]

One of the organisations that has engaged employees in the design, implementation and regular reviews of their Carers' policy is the Scottish Courts and Tribunals Service (SCTS) whose Care Register is referred to in Step 2 above.

---

### Scottish Courts and Tribunals Service Carers' Policy

The SCTS is an independent corporate body established by the Judiciary and Courts (Scotland) Act, 2008. Its function is to provide administrative support to Scottish courts and tribunals and to the judiciary of courts, including the High Court of Justiciary, Court of Session, sheriff courts and justice of the peace courts, and to the Office of the Public Guardian and Accountant of Court. The SCTS Board is chaired by the Lord President, the most senior judge in Scotland.

The SCTS's Carers' policy dates back to an internal working group set up in 2001 (comprising of staff with caring responsibilities, management and the trade union). This generated a far bigger response from staff than had been expected. The working group submitted a report to senior management in May 2002. All seven key recommendations were accepted and implemented. These included the development of a formal Carers' policy, the creation of a Carers' contact team and the establishment of a carer register.

Carers apply through their HR Adviser for inclusion on the SCTS carer register. The HR Adviser arranges an appointment with a welfare officer from the SCTS's independent EAP, who assesses each individual's caring responsibilities before making a recommendation as to whether they should or should not be placed on the register. While staff are encouraged to discuss their application with their line manager, there is no requirement for individuals to disclose the nature of their caring responsibilities with their manager. The SCTS has 219 staff currently on their carer register out of a total workforce of 1,710 full- and part-time staffs, meaning 12.8% of SCTS staff are on the register. A further 190 staffs have been on the register at some point in their careers.

Being placed on the register brings benefits such as:

• financial support for respite care

• interest free loans for the purchase of specialised equipment

• paid special leave for caring commitments.

For many carers, the knowledge that they are supported by the organisation and their line manager is all the benefit they require. Where a manager is supportive it is often much easier for the carer to make a positive contribution at work. The SCTS Carers' policy includes a definition of a carer and sets out clearly what carers should expect from the SCTS. The policy also allows for paid compassionate care leave, where a member of staff requires a longer period off work to care for a terminally ill dependant. All SCTS staff who have passed their probation are entitled to request changes to their terms and conditions — this predates the recent changes to legislation. Currently just under 30% of SCTS staff work part-time hours. The SCTS also operates flexible working hours.

An important implementation element has been the establishment from the outset of a carer contact team (currently nine strong from across the SCTS) made up of current and past employee carers. The team provides valuable peer support to staff, acting as a stepping stone between staff and management or HR as appropriate. The team has expanded its role over the years both promoting the existing Carers' policy and raising new issues. The carer contact team operates as a consultation forum for changes to the Carers' policy and other work-life balance policies (e.g., flexible working hours).

The carer contact team also organises a carer conference every 2 years, which all staffs on the carer register are invited to, along with the person they care for. There have been six well attended conferences to date (most recently in November 2015), each of which was introduced by either the Chief Executive of the SCTS or Lord President at the time. Sessions at previous conferences have included Action on Depression, manual handling, the SCTS-EAP provider and stress handling techniques. At each conference delegates are asked whether SCTS policies still provide support, and are asked for suggestions on improvement. One suggestion from the 2009 conference was provision of free Powers of Attorney to the SCTS staff. The Chief Executive announced at the 2011 conference that the board had agreed to fund Powers of Attorney for all SCTS staffs. The contact team was instrumental in producing a DVD promoting carers in the SCTS, which was filmed in 2013 and launched at that year's conference. The DVD featured an introduction from the then Chief Executive, short presentations from the Director of HR, the chair of the trade union and a carer, and a work-based scenario featuring a typical conversation between a carer and their manager. Copies of the DVD were circulated to all senior managers and it can be viewed on the SCTS carer intranet page.

At the 2015 conference a new SCTS carers intranet forum was launched, where staffs who are carers can share ideas, advice and information. The carer intranet page also contains contact details of the carer contact team, links to other relevant SCTS documents and to a variety of external websites. The carer contact team will be reviewing this page in 2017. The Office of the Public Guardian has developed an action plan following the 2015 conference that includes several proposals to increase recognition of carers in the wider community and improve the service OPG (and therefore SCTS) provides.

In addition to the Carers' policy there is reference to support for carers in the SCTS staff handbook and in a SCTS 'Balancing Life and Work' booklet. There is also 'Benefits for Staff' leaflet which contains a paragraph on the Carers' policy, and which is sent to prospective applicants in external recruitment campaigns. The Carers' register is covered in some depth in the benefits session at Corporate Induction, which all staff are invited to attend, and it is covered in the Managing Stress in Self and Others workshop. In carers' week (see page 101) each year there is an entry in the weekly staff circular promoting the SCTS Carers' policy and register. The Benefits for Staff leaflet is promoted in the weekly staff circular entry each April and October.

Perhaps one reason for the high proportion of employee carers being prepared to identify themselves is that both the current Chief Executive Eric McQueen and his predecessor have been prepared to talk openly to staff about their own caring journeys.

## Carers Networks

Some employers have created carers networks — usually alongside their other employee networks, for example, for women, for employees with disabilities, BME (Black and Minority Ethnic), LGBT, faith groups, etc., EFC estimate that around 1:3 of the EFC members now have networks for employee carers.

The Australian Bureau of Statistics (ABS) Disability and Carers Employee Network was established in early 2014, delivering on an action in the ABS Workplace Diversity Action Plan 2013–2017 to provide support to staff with disability and carers of people with disability. The ABS has offices in each capital city and the network is open to all ABS staff. There are currently around 60 members of the network and new members are regularly encouraged to join via all staff advertisements.

The network meets monthly via video conference, and members discuss work-related matters that may impact on people with disability and caring responsibilities and share personal experiences (for those that want to share). They also provide input into related internal and external initiatives. External guest speakers from carers and disability organisations, selected by network members, are also invited to talk at meetings. The ABS Senior Disability Champion attends the meetings and has helped to raise and address specific workplace-related issues raised at these meetings.

Accenture, a leading global strategy and technology consultancy has had an employee-run network: Accent on Family which has been offered to parents for several years. It runs bespoke events and a buddying scheme for both mothers and fathers returning to work after parental leave. In 2016, it was decided to more explicitly recognise the role that carers play in the activities organised by the Accent on Family programme company wide and now offers a range of activities and events to support carers in Accenture.[119]

## A Typography of Carer Networks

Borrowing a typography developed by the disability rights campaigner and consultant Kate Nash, for disabled employees networks, Carer Employee Networks typically will have one or more of the following functions:

Leadership or champion groups

> These have usually been set up by the organisation itself. They are sometimes called Steering Groups or Advisory Groups (with a membership or interest group mailing list).

> They exist primarily to help the organisation become more carer confident and to raise awareness of the issue across the business or organisation. They are message givers as well as expert advisors and agenda-setters.

Peer group or alumni networks

> These are networks set up primarily by carers themselves usually in response to a growing need for disabled employees to seek peer group support for themselves. They may include personal development and training components in their activities.

Consultation forums

> These are networks set up primarily to act as a consultation group or a forum for the organisation to test out the development of policies, practices and procedures. They may have a formal role to play in consultations.

Most carer networks tend to be hybrids and as Kate Nash notes also of Disabled Employees Networks, may 'start out as one type – reflecting the primary trigger for the network's establishment – but morph, adapt and develop over time to take account of the needs and interests of a range of stakeholders.'[120]

One of the first companies to establish a Carers Network was the international communications company BT (see above page 118). BT already then had a number of other employee networks to learn from: a women's network, an executive women's network, an ethnic minority network, networks for Asian, Muslim and Christian communities; a network for assistants; Able2 –a network for people with disabilities; and Kaleidoscope — a Gay, Lesbian, Bisexual and Transgender network.

The aim of the Carers Network was to provide a single focal point for carers in the company; to build a strong mutual support network building on the collective knowledge and insights of BT's employee carers; to provide links to external networks that have specialist knowledge about caring with people with particular conditions such as dementia. The Carers Network was also designed to provide information links to BT services which might help employee carers such as home-working and emergency leave. It was also envisaged that the Carers Network might identify common issues facing employee carers where BT might be able to provide collective solutions; and that the existence of the network would provide both a route into, and greater credibility with, policy makers.

A senior BT manager — Keith Edwards — who had already emerged as an employee carer through a series of case studies of flexible working arrangements, became the first chairman of the Carers Network. Keith and his wife Jane were caring for their disabled adult daughter Charlotte. Keith ran the network until his retirement in 2014. He did so on a voluntary basis on top of his day job latterly as a Project director and at the start of the network, a General Manager within BT Wholesale.

The Carers Network was promoted through BT's internal newsletters for employees as well as through the news website for employees and the intranet for HR Policies and Practices. A 'Sharepoint' site was set up where employee carers could register their status, post messages and queries/replies and network with fellow carers. Initially, the Carers Network hosted face-to-face workshops but these proved time-consuming and labour-intensive to organise and could reach only a few employees at a time. They soon evolved into online webinars where several hundred employees could register and participate. These 'Knowledge Forums' engaged a series of expert external speakers who were able to participate from their own offices via computer and telephone.[121]

## Credit Suisse Carer Network

In the case of the UK operations of the global financial services company Credit Suisse, two existing, well-established Employee Networks, the Family Network and the Wellness and Accessibility Network saw the need for, and jointly sponsored, a Carers Subgroup, which has grown and evolved in to a full Employee Carers Network over 5 years.

The Carers' network provides:

• Education sessions

• 1:1 support and

• Input to the organisation on policy improvements, for example, carer's leave.

The Carers Network encourages and promotes policies to support carers who are employed by Credit Suisse. By sponsoring the Carers Network as one of its employee networks Credit Suisse demonstrates that it is keen on supporting carers as a key part of its overall Diversity and Inclusion strategy. The Carers Network is also the key promoter of the firm's support of carers to the outside world, for example, through Employees for Carers Networking events. As well as EFC themselves, leaders of Carers Networks at other firms, particularly those similar to Credit Suisse, were a great source of information and inspiration.

The costs of running the Carers' Network are very limited, to cover:

- the time of the staff involved in the network and its steering committee;

- payment for Education session speakers, or donation to their nominated charities;

- printing costs, posters, advertising events and room-hire cross-charges.

A key challenge for the network is securing engagement with the dozens if not hundreds of staff at Credit Suisse who have some kind of caring responsibility. Given the demands of working in a firm like Credit Suisse, employees often find it difficult to attend education sessions during the working day. The convenors try to overcome this with constant promotion of the network and highly visible senior sponsorship (it's OK to be involved with the network because these senior people are ...).

The original Credit Suisse champion for the network was a Managing Director in the firm's front office. As such, she was a very highly visible and senior member of staff. Simply by associating with the network this sponsor lent it a tremendous amount of credibility. She would personally introduce as many of the network lunch time education sessions as she could. This was very powerful and beneficial for these sessions — not only through her seniority but the fact she was in a significant front office (i.e., client facing) role showed that anyone could make time for the events.

The sponsor was active on the firm's UK Diversity Council. This is a senior committee chaired by the UK/EMEA CEO. Having the sponsor on this committee gave the network a tremendous amount of visibility.

In retrospect, three critical success factors for the network were:

1. Membership of Employees for Carers

2. Senior Sponsorship, crucially this is active sponsorship

3. Pulling together a set of Carers Guidelines, highlighting the existing policies the firm has to support carers in the workplace.

More recently, the Carers Network has merged with the Wellness and Accessibility Network and the Mental Health Awareness Group. The intention of this merge is to give the three-employee networks leverage and momentum on the many common objectives they share, particularly around education sessions, while also pooling resources to focus on specific objectives.[122]

My friend, the leading disability rights campaigner Kate Nash, has identified 10 critical success factors for creating and sustaining employee networks.[123] I have consolidated these with the feedback from several chairs/-coordinators of company carer networks that I have interviewed for the book.

### Critical Success Factors for Creating and Sustaining Carer Networks

1. Establish the business case and values: position within the company's overall commitment to diversity and inclusion.

2. Research and engage with other employee networks.

3. Develop clear aims and objectives.

4. Establish clear success criteria and milestones.

5. Secure top-level commitment — preferably a C-suite sponsor.

6. Secure organisational support.

7. Develop the business plan:
   - Structure and status: Being run by carers for carers

   - Proposed activities: Offer time-efficient access to activities like the Knowledge Calls and information that is valued by, and relevant to carers' needs

   - Budget and resources

   - Membership requirements

   - Confidentiality policies.

8. Market the network to employees and communicate across the organisation — making effective use of existing internal company communications channels.

9. Have a dedicated champion (preferably someone who is a carer and can, therefore, talk with authority and expertise on the topic; and develop, support and succession plan for the network coordinators.

**10.** Maintain, develop and review the network — regularly compare notes and exchange learning with the chairs of other in-company Carers Networks.

See also the *EFC guidelines on employee networks for carers.*

---

**Alexis Hay, Standard Life:**

*Having a senior sponsor for the network has been really important.*

Alexis set up a carers network at Standard Life just over a year ago. Numbers have risen quickly: There are now over 140 members in the Edinburgh headquarters with satellite networks starting to spring up in other locations.

When Alexis started the network, she expected members to provide each other with emotional support but has been surprised by the educational side of it. Members have run sessions on subjects ranging from managing incontinence to navigating the benefits system, and use sharepoint to provide members with access to useful information and websites.

Alexis has been given up to half-a-day a week to develop the network, and also has a senior sponsor, Graeme McEwan, who is himself a carer. Alexis says that this senior support has been important (including help from the Standard Life PR team!) and says that the organisation is committed to helping working carers to stay in work.

Standard Life has also been keen to take a lobbying role, engaging with a cross parliamentary group on carers and the Scottish

Executive. It has been awarded a Carers Positive bronze medal by the Scottish government in recognition of its approach and innovative policies. These include offering carers up to 5 days of paid carers leave each year.[124]

There are also clear benefits in the company joining coalitions and employers' networks to share learning and good practice — and thinking about sharing in turn the emerging experience as part of wider corporate responsibility and sustainability knowledge exchanges with suppliers.

## Employers for Carers

Carers UK provides the secretariat and backup for an employer-led network *Employers for Carers*. This began as an employer interest group which emerged during an action-research project led by Carers UK and financed by the *European Social Fund,* from 2002 to 2007 called *Action for Carers and Employment*. Anne Watts, then Head of Diversity and Employee Support at HSBC was first chair of the support group. She recalls: 'the European project was tendered for by Madeleine Starr, a really remarkable researcher. When I was seconded to Business in the Community, I handed on the baton to Caroline Waters at BT'.[125] When the EU project ended, the pioneer employers who had become involved, backed the idea of turning the support group into a subscription-based membership employer network. This began in 2009. It currently involves 120 employers who between them employ more than a million people. EFC is currently the only business-led carers network in the world. See Part 3, Chapter 3, for discussion on how similar employer networks might emerge in other countries.

## STEP 7: MEASURING AND REPORTING

Finally, employers need to measure and report on performance and use this to drive continuous improvement and to trigger further action. Are there targets for increasing the number of employees identifying themselves as carers? For increasing participation in a Carers' Network and take-up of a Carers' Passport where these exist? There is an opportunity for some international human resource management (IHRM) Masters students, IHRM consultants doing pro-bono work or thought-leadership, IHRM professionals or academic experts to analyse corporate responsibility reports over several years to identify both what leading companies are doing and how they are explaining better what they are doing to their stakeholders. This could be an opportunity also to involve some of the Corporate Responsibility coalitions in the employers and carers agenda (see Part 3, Chapter 3).

Some of the data that employers might consider measuring and reporting on, would be:

The number and percentage of eligible/all employees:
- On flexible working
- Taking up Carer leave
- Having a Carer Passport
- Identifying as working carer

o In a Carers' Network

o Returning from care-related leave of absence

o Numbers and percentage of line managers
trained

o Whether there is a Carers policy and carer-
proofing of all HR policies.

The Scottish Courts and Tribunals Service, described
in Step 6 above (page 136) ran a survey of all carers in
the SCTS in June 2014, asking three questions:

o Have you ever benefitted from flexible working arrangements in the SCTS such as those
outlined above for caring reasons?

o Have you ever considered leaving the SCTS
for caring reasons but were able to remain in
work because of these flexible working
arrangements?

o Have you ever requested a change to your
working arrangements in the SCTS for caring
reasons and had this request refused, and
what the reasons for refusal were?

If employers don't measure and report take-up of various flexiwork and other arrangements to help working
carers, we don't know if they are for real. As Anne-Marie
Slaughter writes in *Unfinished Business* (p. 61):

> *In most workplaces, flexi-policies – which range
> from telecommuting and variable work-day sche-
> dules to more radical policies like part-time jobs,
> job sharing, prolonged sabbaticals, or shortened*

*workweeks — exist largely on paper. It is often exceedingly difficult, if not impossible, for employees to avail themselves of them. Indeed, reading through the various studies on this point reminds me of reading through the constitutions of countries behind the Iron Curtain in the former Soviet Union and in dictatorships around the world: they all guaranteed a full panoply of rights and liberties, but only for show.*

*... what academics drily call an 'implementation gap'. In other words, some managers simply refuse to let their employees take advantage of policies on the books, which explains why the National Study of Employers finds a virtual chasm between the percentage of companies that allow some workers to work at home occasionally (67%) and percentage of companies that allow all or most workers to work at home occasionally (8%). The managers who resist change like the workplace culture the way it is based on presence, and hence control, more than on performance. In the words of one HR Manager: when some managers 'can't get someone right there at that particular moment it is actually an uneasy [feeling] for them'.*

I am indebted to the Corporate Responsibility reporting guru Elaine Cohen for good practice examples of employers reporting on their carer policies and practices such as Westpac, already quoted above (page 113).

Effective measurement and reporting is essential if an employer wishes to benchmark their performance against other organisations. In Scotland, the Scottish Government working through Carers Scotland (part of Carers UK) has established the Carer Positive benchmarking service.

## Carer Positive

Carer Positive status is awarded to employers who can provide evidence that they meet criteria in five areas:

1. Identification of carers: There is good understanding of what the term 'carer' means and a system is in place to enable carers to identify themselves.

2. Policy; Carers are recognised within HR policies or procedures.

3. Workplace support: Carers can access practical workplace support or can access information about external support and services.

4. Communication, awareness raising and training: Policies and available support are communicated to all members of staff.

5. Peer support: Carers are supported to engage with other carers.

The award incorporates three levels or stages, from 'engaged' to 'established' through to 'exemplary'. This will enable employers to progress from one stage to the next, building from an initial level of commitment to embedding a culture of support for carers within the organisation. These stages are cumulative, with employers only able to move to the next level once the required criteria at each stage is achieved and maintained. It is assumed that all employers will start at the 'engaged' level unless they can provide evidence that they meet the criteria of the higher levels of achievement.[126]

In New Zealand, Carers New Zealand has established CareWise — a carer-friendly workplace accreditation programme that provides a robust, standardised process to offer practical, cost-effective assistance to employees who have caring responsibilities.

Good management and reporting also enables an employer to compete more effectively for external awards for corporate responsibility, great place to work at — and in turn, such external validation, recognition and kudos helps to build support and awareness internally for organisations, as Centrica, for example, has found.

I asked Caroline Waters — the first chair of EFC — for her tips pm how to become a good employer for working carers.

---

**Caroline Waters' Top 20 Tips for Employers of Carers**

1. Develop and articulate a language that people can understand and crucially can relate to

2. Use the Intranet, social media and other information and communication technologies to find, communicate with, provide lots of practical tips to and encourage collective self-help by employee carers

3. Carer-proof HR policies and practices

4. Create a specific Carer Policy

5. Establish a Carer Passport scheme

6. Offer flexible working

7. Involve carers and especially ex-carers as champions, mentors and trainers for employee carers and their colleagues

8. Find and deploy high-profile company Carers' champions who will speak authentically and personally about working, caring and living

9. Show line managers how being accommodating and helpful to employee carers does not have to make it harder to achieve commercial goals

10. Train line managers appropriately, for example, to understand that someone caring for a loved one with degenerative condition will typically need periodic readjustments to their Carer Passport

11. Create and support an in-house Carers network

12. Have policies and practices for re-integrating ex-carers including training line managers to learn how to reframe their views of ex-carers when they cease caring

13. Be proactive: Help employees prepared to become carers

14. Segment your employee carers by the type of caring they are doing

15. Advise colleagues of ex-carers about being sympathetic and emotionally intelligent

16. Share learning about supporting employee carers internally and externally and learn from others

17. Build alliances with strategic partner organisations

18. Develop your business case for supporting carers

19. Identify and advocate for public policy changes that will help employee carers: encourage Carers to tell their own stories widely — including to politicians and opinion

formers to ensure the latter remain aware of key issues outside the workplace that may prevent employee mobility. For example, difference in care provision across councils may prevent a carer taking an opportunity if it means the cared for person might experience a break or reduction in their experience of local services

20. Join EFC (or equivalent network in other countries).

## FOCUS ON THE 5PS

Some organisations value a simple 'memory-jogger'/ checklist to help them care for their carers and to explain what they are doing. So, here are the 5Ps for being a great employer for working carers.

| | |
|---|---|
| PREPARATION | – Identify working carers |
| | – Consult them on what would be most helpful and on how best to find hidden carers |
| | – Look at what other employers are doing for their working carers |
| POLICY | – Carer-proof existing policies such as flexible working and leave |
| | – Adopt a specific Carer Policy, cross-referencing to other HR policies and practice |
| | – Introduce Carer Leave |
| PROMOTION | – Use existing externally-organised events such as a Carers Rights Day or Carers Week (where they exist) to promote Carer policy — or help to create such profile-raising events |
| | – Publicise support for carers through regular communications with employees |

|            | – Encourage leaders to 'come out' about their own caring roles |
|------------|---------------------------------------------------------------|
| PRACTICE   | – Introduce a Carer Passport                                  |
|            | – Include emergency backup care for if employee's regular (elder)care arrangements break down |
|            | – Make reasonable adjustments such as reserved parking spaces or allowing use of mobile phone for carers |
|            | – Provide advice and information for carers on the organisation's intranet, link to external help such as carers' organisations and condition-specific charities which also offer help to carers of someone with the condition |
|            | – Train line managers on caring for carers and how to raise the issue sensitively with their direct reports and their reports |
| PEER SUPPORT | – Create/support an employee carers network, alongside networks for disabled, LGBT, etc. |
|            | – Exchange learning and experience with other employers informally or through representative employer groups and/or dedicated networks of employers of carers. |

## Just a Big Organisation Issue? Caring and SMEs

So far, the organisations discussed have been medium to large size. Many people, however, work for small enterprises. Intriguingly, in The United States, 17% of working carers are self-employed or own their own business versus 9.4% of The United States workforce overall. The issues involved in juggling work and care are just the same, but the organisational responses may be different. Smaller organisations may not have the time or the need to develop formal policies. Like for many other topics, smaller organisations will rely on a general organisational culture and philosophy — and use those to respond to particular circumstances and needs as they arise. As Simon Hodgson, one of the founding partners of the 25-person independent management consultancy Carnstone Partners LLP explained: 'like lots of small and medium enterprises (SMEs), we make our road by walking. So we have made up our caring "policy" as we have gone along. For us, it is a matter of culture: What kind of organisation we want to be. We talk a lot about our culture and how we would handle different circumstances. We have had to handle several caring situations such as end-of-life care for a parent. We try and be as flexible as possible with options of discretionary paid leave and unpaid leave. So far, we have found that colleagues have wanted to carry on doing some work. It is good for their state of mind. For the business it is very simple: We depend totally on the quality of our people and of their relationships with clients. Our biggest constraint is finding good staff so losing a good person would be very painful for us. There is a business case for us to be flexible and supportive. So our aim is ensure colleagues can bring their whole selves to work. When there have been caring situations, we have been totally transparent with clients and they have been enormously supportive'.[127]

---

### Listawood

Listawood is a small business, with a workforce of around 150 people, which manufactures promotional products such as ceramic mugs, fridge magnets and mouse pads; and is based in King's Lynn, eastern England. The company has made a firm commitment to creating a culture of flexibility and support for those needing to balance their home and work lives, often at short notice, which they believe is a significant driver of their strong record of staff retention.

The recent recession, and increased competition from emerging low-wage economies has placed enormous strain on Listawood's sector, creating pressure to keep staff costs low. As part of their performance management framework, Listawood regularly surveys their employees to measure staff satisfaction. The company are aware that they do not offer the best salary levels in the area — indeed only 56% of staff surveyed felt their pay was competitive when compared with other employers locally. However their deep rooted culture of flexibility is well recognised by staff — 97% felt that the company offered better opportunities for work-life balance than other employers in the area.

Explaining their approach, Listawood Managing Director Alex Turner says: 'Losing highly trained staff is incredibly disruptive in any business. In the sales environment it fractures customer relationships which can result in reduced levels of business, and in the factory it compromises of manufacturing efficiency. On top of this you then have to bear the costs associated with recruitment and training for their replacement. We are in no doubt that our staff retention levels are driven by our attitude to work-life balance rather than the generosity of our remuneration packages. This makes it possible for us to remain competitive and profitable in a highly competitive market, even during these unusually difficult trading conditions'.[128]

There is a very similar attitude in the responses of several small enterprises on the business transparency and accountability reporting website Responsible 100 (www.responsible100.com), to the question: 'Does your company have a policy or arrangement in place that allows for carers to balance work with their care responsibilities?'[129] None of the small businesses responding there do have a formal policy.

However as *Pukka Herbs*, the organic herbal tea and supplement company, founded in 2001 explains: 'One of our stated Pukka Values is to be open and we foster a culture whereby individuals can discuss their personal circumstances with their line manager or the People Manager. New team members are introduced to our values and policies as part of their induction programme. We understand that team members have responsibilities outside of their employment and if time off work is required for this, we try to accommodate it and have done so, despite not having a formal arrangement. For longer term caring responsibilities, employees may request flexible working through their line manager and this will be considered and granted if possible. A formal policy covering this is currently in draft form. Our sustainability introduction to new team members includes our commitment to supporting a work-life balance and the possibility of flexible working to balance work with care responsibilities'.

Some respondents suggest how they would adapt from their existing approach to childcare: 'As Green Stationery only have four staff, we have not yet had any need to develop a specific policy for carers. However, an option is available to all employees to adopt flexible hours, as and when their needs dictate. One member of staff leaves 2 hours earlier than others due to childcare duties'.

Similarly, BE INSPIRED FILMS explains: 'As a small business this is not something we have encountered and as such do not have policies in place for employees who are also carers. All of our staff are self-employed associates and often work from home in their own time, which means they can work flexibly at times that suit them as long as the work is completed on time. Some of our staff have recently had children and we have made a conscious effort to adapt working practices so that they can balance the added responsibilities of home life and childcare with work responsibilities and have more time for their families. An example of this is scheduling film days to work around childcare and also adding in buffer time around deadlines so that stress levels and late-night working are limited. We feel confident that should we have an employee who had additional caring responsibilities, we would be able and very happy to make similar adjustments to support them in managing both their responsibilities. In the future we would like to formalise this as we grow'.

Very often, the needs of employee carers can be met simply by some management creativity. Grosser Cleaning and Care Services based in Frechen, Germany provides domestic cleaning and personal care services for the aging population. The company works with employees to arrange work schedules around their family's needs, whether those entail childcare or informal care for their relatives. This kind of flexibility in work hours allows employees to navigate changes not only in family circumstances but also in their own health status, without needing to resign from their jobs.[130]

*Happy Ltd* (a training company with 35 employees) has found that its relatively small size and lack of formal procedures have helped rather than hindered it to try innovative working arrangements: 'We will consider any request to work flexibly and we don't make any judgement on the reasons why. We are creating a great culture and it is "can do" rather than "can't." We don't want an organisation where people are treated differently. We have an ethic of fairness, dignity and respect'. Following one member of staff needing extra dependency leave and another needing extra carer's leave, the company has also introduced 10 paid days of dependency/carers leave after 5 years of service.

*Associe International INC.* is a small Japanese nursery company that has won the prize from Tokyo metropolitan authority as an advanced company for supporting employees' combining work and elderly care.

One option for a small enterprise is to look out for and join a local network of SME employers which is sharing experience and good practice either specifically on work and caring, or more broadly on great workplace practices. See Part 3, Chapter 3, for more details.

James Ashwell, who quit his job to care for his mum with dementia (page 35), had wanted to start his own business since he was a kid. It was caring for his mum for 5 years that gave him the idea of sourcing and selling products suitable for people living with dementia. As he found ways to cope with the stress and challenges and enjoy moments of happiness and connection, James found a passion he never knew he possessed: to discover great products to help other people affected by dementia to cope better. After his mum died, Ashwell created *Unforgettable.* Today he is pursuing his twin passions: to run his own sustainable business and to improve the quality of life for those living with dementia and their carers. Unforgettable has attracted investments from some of the heavy weights of impact investing such as Bridges Ventures and IVUK (Impact Venture UK). James describes Unforgettable as 'a beautiful business' — the Unforgettable Foundation has a golden share ensuring the protection of the business's social mission both now and in the future; and the Unforgettable constitution — the memorandum and articles of association — set out the history and philosophy of the business. Unforgettable has already become one of the first of 2,000 pioneer B-Corps across the world. B-Corps have an explicit societal purpose and have to meet stretching social, environmental and economic impact criteria. To achieve B-Corps status, candidate businesses must score at least 80 points on the B-Corps certification process. Unforgettable scored 112 but when I met James, he was already looking to improve on that score when Unforgettable is reaccredited.[131]

The specialist agency *Miracle Workers* which I used to recruit my mum's live-in carers (see Introduction page xlii) began when founder Miriam Warner was looking for quality carers for her own mum.

Ollie Black was in brand management with FMCG global giant *Procter & Gamble* (by coincidence where I also started after university — albeit many years earlier!). He saw the positive impact that having good childcare made to the people working in the business, but also how difficult it was for parents to arrange good, local childcare. Convinced that childcare in The United Kingdom was about to go through massive change, he built up a childcare business along with his brother Ben and friend Amanda. This subsequently expanded into My Family Care: www.myfamilycare.co.uk as corporate clients started asking more and more for support for employees with eldercare as well as childcare issues.

## Future-Friendly Workplaces

Employers and employees may find it easier to instigate carer-friendly policies and practices in working environments which already recognise very different employment patterns to the past. In *The alliance: Managing Talent in the Networked Age,* co-founder and chairman of LinkedIn Reid Hoffman and his co-authors Ben Casnocha and Chris Yeh describe a new model of employer-employee relations that is becoming popular in Silicon Valley. The authors start from the premise that the lifetime employment model and the employee loyalty that this generated is dead. Millennial workers understand very well that they will hold many jobs over the course of their careers, leading them to limit their investment in their employers just as their employers have little incentive to invest in them. *The Alliance* proposes a very different model in which both sides, as the name suggests, ally to advance their mutual interests. In this model, job contracts are not seen as open-ended commitments but as 'tours of duty' that have clearly defined goals and finite time spans. After your tour is up, you might go on to another tour within the same company or go to another company entirely. Tours of duty could fit much better with periods off or part-time working for caring.

I am a huge fan of the book '*The 100 year life*'[132] by Lynda Gratton and Andrew Scott from the London

Business School. They argue that increasing longevity means the old three-stage model of education-work-retirement is redundant; and that instead we should anticipate periods of renewal to recharge our batteries, refresh our skills or to acquire entirely new skills for a career shift. Increasing longevity, Gratton and Scott argue, makes it all the more important for individuals to build up not just their tangible assets: property, pension pot, other savings; but also crucially their intangible assets: loving family and close friends; extensive circles of contacts and acquaintances and the like. If you are living longer and working longer (albeit potentially in very different ways) it is much easier to foresee times out of the labour market for periods of extended travel or to pursue a sport or hobby, or to go back to studying. In such a future-orientated work environment, natural life-stages like time out for caring for a parent or a parent-in-law should feel much more part of the normal cycle of life and of working life and employers should adjust to this.

## TAKE-AWAY

Even amongst the 50 + employers quoted here, there is not a consensus on the right approach to helping employee carers. Some employers proactively seek out their employee carers; others treat this as strictly a matter for individual choice whether to reveal caring responsibilities. Some have formal carer policies linked to broader flexible working and leave policies. Others rely on general policies or even on an empowering and supportive culture. Some have Carer Passports and carer leave; others rely on ad hoc arrangements. One size clearly does not fit all. The most effective arrangements will be those that reconcile with overall organisational culture. Nevertheless, there are some key take-aways:

Leadership by example

Supportive and empowered line management

Willingness to adapt flexibly to changing individual circumstances

A long-term shared destiny relationship rather than a transactional one so that there is a more sophisticated 'give and take' mind-set.

# PART 3

---

# BUILDING A MOVEMENT

*IT'S NOT IF,*

*IT'S WHEN*

*YOU WILL*

*BE A CARER*

— *Carers Canada*

# CHAPTER 1

# BECOMING A CHAMPION EMPLOYER OF CARERS

*More employers are starting to recognise and support working carers but they remain a minority. Whilst the priority must be to engage many more employers in many more countries around the world, it is already possible to speculate on some of the dimensions of policies and practise required to be a champion: a great employer of carers. This would include continuous improvement in, and high rates of take-up by both male and female employees of, carer policies. Champion employers, however, would also be using their influence throughout their value chain to engage suppliers including freelancers and also customers. They would be preparing their employees for future caring responsibilities, and proactively examining the use of digital technologies to support working carers. As workforces age, champions will promote returnships for ex-carers to re-join the labour market. Champion employers would also leverage their experience and commitment to get 'a seat at the table' in public policy discussions about how better to help carers, including working carers.*

For the past decade, my 'day job' has been as professor of Corporate Responsibility (CR) and Director of the Doughty Centre for CR at Cranfield University School of Management — one of the world's top business schools. Cranfield is just one of only 74 out of the 13,000 + business schools in the world to hold the triple 'crown' accreditation from the most sought-after international accreditations from the leading business schools ratings agencies: AACSB (The Association to Advance Collegiate Schools of Business), AMBA (International Association of MBAs), EQUIS. I am not an academic by training. I joined the world of management education at the age of 52 years and although I don't have a PhD, Cranfield gave me a professorship in CR based on several decades' experience of working with businesses large and small, in The United Kingdom and internationally.

## WHAT DOES 'CORPORATE RESPONSIBILITY' MEAN FOR EMPLOYERS OF CARERS?

There are many different definitions of CR. One recent academic study identified 37 different definitions for CR (Dahlsrud, 2008). Howard Bowen in 'Social Responsibilities of the Businessman' (1953) asked: 'what responsibilities to society can business people be reasonably expected to assume?' and described CR as 'the obligations of businessmen to pursue those policies, to make those decisions, or to follow those lines of action which are desirable in terms of the objectives and values of our society'.

The American Academic Archie Carroll, defines Corporate Social Responsibility: in the Evolution of a Definitional Construct (1979), as 'social responsibilities of business encompasses the economic, legal, ethical and discretionary expectations that society has of organisations at *a given point*'. I would emphasise Carroll's last four words. He rightly stresses that society's expectations evolve over time. Executive pay, corporate tax strategies, how companies lobby, would be examples of this evolution over the past decade.

I particularly like the European Commission definition from October 2011:

'... the responsibility of enterprises for their impacts on society'.[133]

I passionately believe that business can be a force for good; that business should have a societal purpose beyond just making a profit; and that business has a licence to operate from society that will be restricted or expanded, depending on how it behaves. Some set this in the context of creating a more responsible, inclusive and sustainable capitalism.

## Stages of Corporate Responsibility Maturity

Whenever I am asked by students and journalists, whether businesses are taking their responsibilities more seriously, I invariably answer that there is a wide variety of responses. Organisations are at different stages of CR maturity.

- Stage 1 Denier — not recognising any responsibility for a company's Social, Environmental and Economic (SEE) impacts;

- Stage 2 Complier — following laws and common business practices in dealing with SEE impacts;

- Stage 3 Risk Mitigator — identifying material SEE impacts and reducing negative impacts to mitigate reputational, financial, regulatory, social 'licence to operate' risks;

- Stage 4 Opportunity Maximiser — reducing negative SEE impacts but also now systematically seeking business opportunities from optimising positive impacts the business has;

- Stage 5 Champion — both embracing sustainability in its own value-chain, but also collaborating with others and advocating public policy changes to create sustainable development.[134]

In the previous chapter, I suggested how employers could at least mitigate risks and preferably become net positive, and create mutually beneficial opportunities as a good employer of carers. It will need time, but we might envisage some employers evolving to a 'Champion' stage of CR — at least when it comes to being a great employer for working carers.

This might, for example, involve:

- Clearly linking carer policies and practices to the organisation's societal purpose;

- Taking a consistent leadership role over time both internally and externally in organisations helping other employers to develop their own carer policies and practices;

— Actively engaging their value-chain (business customers and suppliers) in dialogue about their own carer policies and practices; and supporting them to improve their performance vis-à-vis employee carers — and in particular, supporting their freelance contractors — see Chapter 2 below;

— Sharing their experiences and details of carer policies and practices, training programmes, resources such as Carer Passports, with other employers through speaking at workshops and conferences;

— Helping their own former employees and others who had to quit the job market in order to care full-time, to go back to work as/if their circumstances change;

— Advising governments on how to create more of an enabling environment for working and caring;

— Sponsoring independent research and awards to identify and promote good practice in carer policies and practices.

One employer already doing many of these things is Centrica: see box.

---

### CENTRICA

CENTRICA is a top 30 FTSE company. Although predominantly a UK business, it also has a significant presence in North America. It has 37,000 employees and a four generation workforce.

Centrica, owner of British Gas, has done more than most to support carers and retain their skills.

It started to support carers earlier than many employers. It has had a *carers network* since 2005 and the network now has more than a 1,000 members and for many years a senior business sponsor, Ian Peters, who is a key supporter of Carers UK and Employers for Carers. (see Foreword page xxiii).

It plays an important role in *awareness raising* about Centrica's *carers' leave policy* and carers' needs. Centrica's carers' policies cover those with elder care responsibilities, or a disabled child, but not childcare for which it has separate policies. Close friends, as well as family members, who are primary carers are included in the scheme.

A growing number of employees have both childcare and eldercare responsibilities, says Alison Hughes, then head of human resources policy and diversity, adding that it may be more difficult to predict eldercare needs which can sometimes be unplanned.

Centrica's policy has been running for more than a decade and it remains one of only a few large companies to offer paid leave for carers. There is no 'time-served' requirement. Centrica's innovative carer's leave policy provides up to 1 month of matched leave. Employees tend to take a couple of days at a time, for instance to attend hospital appointments. They can take longer periods for such responsibilities as nursing someone after a serious illness. Half the time off is taken as carers' leave, half as annual holiday.

Alison Hughes says many carers don't need to take several weeks off. They may, however, need a few days at a time on several occasions in a year, for instance, to make long-term care arrangements. Due to Centrica's *flexible working policy* many carers don't have to take leave, but can adjust their working times and, for instance, leave early. 2,200 employees took carers leave in 2014.

Employees have 24/7 access to advice and information about caring through Centrica's *independently-provided Employee Assistance Programme (EAP)*.

Centrica forecasts that 60% of its 36,000-strong workforce will also be carers during their working lives. It points to research that suggests that working carers who have to tackle an unsupportive environment are five times more likely to experience stress and unplanned absence.

*Business benefits of supporting carers.* By helping staff to combine work with caring responsibilities, it estimates that it saves £4.5 million a year in absenteeism and £2 million by retaining staff who would otherwise have to be replaced, at the cost of extra recruitment and training. It also estimates annual savings of £10 million on recruitment costs. One in five UK carers has to give up work to meet caring responsibilities, says Carers UK. Centrica says it is unaware of any of its staff having done so since it introduced its policy.

'It's not just about us being a good employer, it's looking forward', says Alison Hughes. The policy improves not only the well-being of staff members, she adds, but also their commitment to the company. Indeed British Gas (BG) margins on the work of its 12,000 engineers are three times higher than those of the nearest competitor because BG engineers have been with the company long-term and are, therefore, very skilled and experienced. Retention has required offering very flexible work patterns.

In 2014, Centrica set up a *Pilot Training Programme for Managers* in BG call-centres, with Working Families and Employers for Carers which was focused on carers and flexible working. The hook for the programme was the extension of the right to request flexible working to all employees. Those taking part were managers who had people with CRs in their teams. The rationale was that if line-managers have 10–11 people reporting to them, then statistically they will have at least one carer in their team.

'One thing that resonates with a lot of managers is that this isn't like having a family, which typically you would choose to do. Caring happens to you and it can happen overnight', says Alison Hughes.

Centrica is looking at embedding this in its line manager training programme. 'We are trying to embed diversity and inclusion and flexible working is a part of this. We have found that stand alone modules don't make a difference to day-to-day working', says Alison. 'It's all about being a good manager and promoting team-building and good behaviour. There is no single solution to these issues. We need to create the right culture'. That also includes having good role models, including of senior managers who are working flexibly.

More recently, Centrica has launched a *new returner initiative with Mars and Vodafone*, which recognises the often overlooked talent pool of mainly women who have taken career breaks for family reasons and want to get back to work.

The returner initiative, which has received a lot of support internally, including from Centrica's employee networks, is a pilot programme and the first cross-business one between Centrica, Mars and Vodafone. The organisations involved are now considering what a wider roll out may look like.

Alison Hughes says it is clear there is a lot of value in the programme, which is open to men and women, and she says the cross-business nature of it is powerful. It came out of a roundtable event at the Women's Business Council, of which all three companies are members. 'Having three big brands on board was very attractive', Alison adds.

The response rate has been good. Alison cites one woman who had been out of the workplace for over 10 years who was interviewed for a big operational role. 'She has fantastic experience and leadership. She blew us away', she says.

Centrica will be modifying the programme in-line with what it has learnt and with a continued focus on the Thames Valley/M4 corridor, where it has its Headquarter (HQ) near London's Heathrow Airport. For instance, it has decided to take people on according to the talent gaps across different departments in the organisation in-line with its annual capability review.

The focus on returners is all part of Centrica's talent attraction and retention strategy, which includes embedding a diversity lens in talent metrics, particularly around gender, and mentors to support female talent.

The *employee networks*, which grow organically and are employee-led, are using YAMMER (which can now go to smart phones); and also linking up more. Besides carers these networks include parents, women's and LGBT (lesbian, gay, bisexual or trans) networks. They have quarterly meetings to share what they have learnt as well as resources, for instance, one network might attend or speak at another network's event.

### British Gas Employee Carer Network

*Geoff Kitchener* Centrica Carers Network National Chair

The BG Carers' Network began life in November 2004 with e-mails sent to all known employee carers in BG, asking them if they would be prepared to help build the network. It was formally launched in 2005 and in the first couple of years existed in name only, with local groups operating at a number of BG locations, including the Staines HQ, Edinburgh, Cardiff, Leeds and Stockport. In 2007, there was an awareness raising campaign and the creation of a national database of carers. Geoff Kitchener, who has cared for his wife Rosanne since 2001 and who had chaired the Edinburgh Carers Group from the outset, became national chair.

Today, the BG Carers' Network has over 1,000 members, but as Kitchener points out, with 18,000–19,000 employees, that means less than half of all BG employee carers have come forward. 'There's still a lot of hidden carers. The Network uses external events like the annual Carers Week in June, to seek out BG's hidden carers'.

The BG Carers' Network provides help and advice; and sometimes also mediates where an employee carer has grievances with line management or human resource (HR). Carers have a dedicated area on the BG Intranet. There is a page for asking questions and seeking advice. There is also a CNet Yammer within BG's Yammer service.

There is a strong connection to the BG Well-being hub, which has advice and information on exercising regularly, eating healthily and work-life balance, all things which are often sacrificed by employee carers, who frequently give up watching out for their own physical and mental well-being in the face of job and caring priorities.

For Kitchener, it remains an ongoing challenge to keep awareness raising going; to regularly recharge and refresh the network. Looking ahead to his own retirement in 2020, Kitchener is already thinking about succession planning.

*********************

Centrica has also invested in an *online portal* and tailored to the company's needs.

Another area for future development is *support for older workers*. 'What we offer in terms of family support is not just about parents or carers. It's end-to-end resources for families', says Alison. 'We want to create an inclusive culture so people can bring their whole selves to work'.

## PREPARING 'WILL-BES' — EMPLOYEES WHO WILL BE CARING IN THE FUTURE

Champions will be at the forefront of a future drive to shift from a reactive, 'seat of the pants', approach to caring, to a more prepared, proactive approach. In other words, champions will show how to prepare the 'will-bes', the future carers. 'Fore-warned is fore-armed', the saying goes — and it is true. I have lost count of the number of carers who have said to me, 'if only I had known at the beginning of my caring journey, what I know now, it would have been so much easier and I would have been so much better a carer'. It is something I feel strongly myself. Clearly, being heavy-handed or adopting a negative, over-scary tone, would be counter-productive. Presented thoughtfully, however, employers could play a valuable role in prompting 'will-bes' to think ahead, discuss options with those affected, better spot 'early warning' signs that caring might be on the horizon, and build knowledge about where advice and information is available, for when it becomes relevant.

## HARNESSING THE DIGITAL REVOLUTION TO CARE FOR CARERS BETTER

There is a really neat animation on YouTube: 'The Evolution of the Desk 1980—2014', which shows how a typical office-worker's desk has changed over the past few years as diaries, calculators, rolladexes, family photos and the like have all gradually been replaced by apps on our computer desktops.[135]

We have lived through an astounding rate of technological change. It is now a well-repeated truism that your smart phone is millions of times more powerful that all of NASA's combined computing in 1969, and that an *iPhone* could be used to guide 120,000,000 Apollo era spacecraft to the moon, all at the same time'.[136] In so many ways, these technology changes have brought huge benefits for most of us.

Now, experts in the World Economic Forum and elsewhere talk of the *Fourth Industrial Revolution* that will 'fundamentally alter the way we live, work and relate to one another. In its scale, scope and complexity, the transformation will be unlike anything humankind has experienced before'. It is characterised by a fusion of technologies that is blurring the lines between the physical, digital and biological spheres.[137]

The Fourth Industrial revolution will bring many exciting benefits. It is also, however, carries huge risks and downsides. A report by the global consulting firm Accenture for The United Kingdom responsible business coalition *Business in the Community 'A Brave New World? Why business must ensure an inclusive Digital Revolution' (Accenture for BITC November 2016)* highlights potential benefits from the Digital Revolution such as helping to reduce inequalities and improve livelihoods; creating new jobs, enhancing societal outcomes: such as saving lives (through assisted driving); enhancing environmental outcomes; opening up education; and enabling smarter working (eg remotely).

'A Brave New World?' also, however, highlights the potential downsides of the Digital Revolution. 'Forecast job losses due to automation range significantly' the report notes, '– one prediction suggests as many as 10 million job losses in The United Kingdom by 2035'. Many older workers may find it hard to acquire the necessary new skills for the new jobs that will be available. Digital technologies can also reduce face-to-face contact, which can in turn 'have mental health impacts and increase loneliness'. This danger particularly resonated as I read the Accenture-BitC report immediately after reading a challenging speech by Julia Unwin the retiring Chief Executive of the Joseph Rowntree Foundation (JRF) on the future of Civil Society, in which she quotes a respondent to a JRF loneliness programme:

*I'd really like to talk to someone who wasn't paid to talk to me.*[138]

Accenture and BitC are very clear: 'Business has the opportunity to help secure an inclusive digital revolution'. The report highlights three areas of significant opportunity.

Opportunity 1: Enabling the rapid transition of employees from traditional jobs to the high-quality jobs of the future, building digital skills, actively managing job losses (there are analogies to where BitC started in the 1980s with local enterprise agencies, job-creation initiatives like British Coal Enterprise, British Steel Industry, etc.); and proactively seeking to open up new jobs to under-represented groups: women, older workers, etc.

Opportunity 2: Ensuring that digital technology is used to enhance transparency of business practices and operations, building trust with consumers and wider stakeholders, for example, using digital-to-drive transparency across supply chains and managing personal data of customers responsibly. I would add employees, and also add the responsibility to protect the data securely against cyber-attack, cyber-fraud, etc. Indeed, other Accenture authors have written extensively on Corporate Digital Responsibility: 'Guarding and growing personal data value' (https://www.accenture.com/gb-en/insight-guarding-growing-personal-data-value).

Opportunity 3: Finding new ways to deliver social and environmental benefits while creating business value. 'A Brave New World?' argues that 'The opportunities that digital transformation creates for radically different ways of doing business can drive societal benefits including reducing environmental footprints, enabling Internet access for all and enhancing community cohesion, all while creating new value for the private sector'. The report notes that digital solutions play a critical role in more than 50% of the 169 targets that sit beneath the United Nations' 17 Sustainable Development Goals, adopted in 2015, while offering around £7 trillion in additional revenues and reduced costs.

Individual major companies are using information and communication technologies, and insights about on-line learning, and virtual meetings to co-create and share new insights about improving profitability and sustainability performance, for and with their extended supply chains. 2-degrees, the online community for sustainability professionals, for example, has provided branded knowledge-sharing platforms to individual companies such as Tesco and ASDA Walmart. These platforms provide virtual meeting spaces, online matchmaking between people seeking solutions and solutions-providers, virtual libraries of know-how and know-who. They are backed up with sophisticated user-profiles both of participating suppliers and of individual employees in these companies. A key part of the added-value that the 2-degrees platform provides are the protocols and good practice guidance, for example, governing sensitive issues such as protecting details of cost-savings generated through the supplier knowledge interchange.[139]

This model could be adapted by champion employers to support other organisations in their value chain (both suppliers and business/organisational customers) to develop their own support for working carers.

In April 2014, The National Alliance for Caregiving in The United States convened an expert roundtable with a panel of 22 national experts from Silicon Valley, government agencies, and the non-profit sector, to examine whether technology can play a more meaningful role in helping caregivers? And how to accelerate innovation in developing new applications to support caregivers?

The round-table identified a number of critical issues (Diagram 1)

It concluded that 'Technology-based solutions have the potential to lighten the burden that falls on family

**Diagram 1: Successful Caregiving Technologies Require Three Supports.**

| Successful Caregiving Technologies | | |
| --- | --- | --- |
| **Framing the Issues** | **Creating a Fertile Environment** | **Maximizing the Value** |
| • Mapping the landscape | • Spurring a national conversation | • Coaching complements technology |
| • Creating shared language | • Developing business cases | • Inspiring social conversations |
| • Collecting relevant data | | |

*Source*: Reproduced with permission from The National Alliance for Caregiving.

caregivers, particularly by helping them to coordinate the demanding tasks and the complex networks of relationships involved with caring for others. Technology could also help improve the health of both caregivers and care recipients'.[140]

The Digital Revolution could help employers to champion significant improvements in caring for working carers. Firstly, digital working can help employees juggling working and caring:

> More flexible working patterns will be critical. Twenty per cent of the over 50s in the UK are carers — many of them end up leaving the workforce because they cannot combine an inflexible job with caring responsibilities. (Andy Briggs, CEO, Aviva UK and Ireland Life, Chairman of Global Life and Chair of Business in the Community's Age at Work Leadership Team)[141]

Secondly, digital technology enables employers to target relevant, customised information to subgroups of their working carers such as a podcast about new tools for those caring for someone living with dementia; or the availability of carer respite services for employees in specific geographic locations.

Thirdly, digital technologies enhance opportunities for carer networks to organise virtual meetings and chatrooms providing peer-support.

Champion employers could play a convening and leadership role in pursuing this technology and caring agenda.

## RETURNSHIPS

Champion employers will be thinking not just about retaining existing carers in their workplace, but also being proactive about returnships — helping people who have given up work to care, to get back into a job, if their caring journey has come to an end as Centrica are doing together with Vodafone and Mars.

A returnship is a professional internship designed specifically for people (usually women) returning after an extended career break. It's a short-term position drawing on existing skills and experience, and may be supplemented with relevant training courses. It gives a chance for the returner to build their confidence and gain recent CV experience, while practically testing out the role and whether they want to return to a demanding corporate job. From the employer's side, they have access to the skills of an experienced professional and a low-risk way of assessing the returner as a potential longer-term employee. *Goldman Sachs* in The United States (which trademarked the term 'returnship' in 2008) has been running a programme since 2010, initially in New York and now also in India. It's for professionals looking to restart their careers after 2 + years out (average 6 years). The paid 10-week programme offers work experience in a variety of departments, with real business issues to work on, together with an induction and a range of courses such as self-promotion, influence and industry trends. Goldman state that around 50% of participants have gone on to full-time roles. J.P. Morgan, Morgan Stanley, and Credit Suisse have also offered such programmes. Another well-established returnship programme is in

India, where since 2008 the conglomerate *Tata Group* have been running their Second Career Internships. They offer a residential induction and 500 hours of flexitime projects spread over 6 months to professional women who have taken 1–8 year break. Tata states that the majority of participants have subsequently returned to the workforce.

*Path Forward* is an independent non-profit, founded in The United States in 2016 whose aim is to help companies set up mid-career internships for individuals — parents and other caregivers — who've been out of the workforce for a few years. The non-profit will help corporations' HR departments set up mid-career internships — for a flat fee — with a few parameters in mind. The internships are to be 20-week, paid positions available to individuals — both men and women — who have been out of the professional workforce for at least 2 years to care for children, a spouse, or a parent. The hope is that employers will hire interns as full-time workers at the end of the temporary stint. Companies will choose whom to hire for their programs, but Path Forward's website will serve as a database for all the available positions.[142]

There is obviously potential here to apply the learning from groups like Path Forward to returning ex-carers.

## CHAMPION EMPLOYERS AS PUBLIC POLICY ADVOCATES

A major factor leading many working carers to give up work — however supportive their employer is — can be the unavailability, inadequacy, unreliability and/or inefficiency of professional care and health services and support. A recent survey for Carers UK, showed that 30% of carers who had given up work, retired early or reduced working hours had done so because there were no suitable care services available, and 22% because care services were too expensive.[143]

Links between caring and labour market withdrawal are less pronounced in countries where more formal services are available.[144]

Some employers of carers, therefore, may decide that, in order to ensure their own carer policy is effective, they need to advocate for good quality health and care services as well. A champion employer of carers may thus get involved in government taskforces or encourage Senior Managers to join the Board of a local Public Health Service for an area where the employer has a concentration of employees, in order to secure improvements in publicly-provided health and care services.

Effective employer policies and practices and advocacy work, will support each level of the pyramid of carer needs (Prof Janet Fast) (**Diagram 2**).

A champion employer might also commission think-tanks to research/lobby for fiscal and/or regulatory changes, or programme innovations to build a private/ third sector provided care-market. This might involve public policy advocacy for something like the Belgian or French schemes to incentivise the care market, described below in Part 3 — Chapter 3 (page 205).

Champions might even get directly involved in schemes to build a market for respite care like the New Zealand Mycare on-line platform: www.mycare.co.nz.

**Diagram 2:  Janet Fast Pyramid of Carer Needs.**

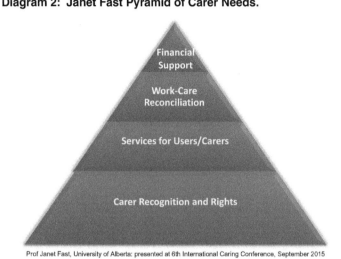

Prof Janet Fast, University of Alberta: presented at 6th International Caring Conference, September 2015

## TAKE-AWAY

'Champion' employers — highly responsible businesses supporting working carers in their organisations — could undertake a variety of measures, including carer policies aligned with business purpose and culture; exercising leadership inside and outside their organisations to engage, share knowledge and support other employers as well as customers and suppliers to develop their own carer programmes; exploit new technologies to support working carers; become advocates for governments to create more of an enabling environment for working and caring; and sponsor independent research and awards to identify and promote good practice in carer policies and practices.

# CHAPTER 2

## WHEN THE CARER IS THEIR OWN BOSS — SUPPORTING FREELANCERS

*Take Care is about how employers can take care of their employee carers. What happens, however, if you are your own boss: if you are self-employed? As we saw at the outset, almost 1:5 American working carers are freelancers or run their own businesses. Going self-employed is the route for many working carers who want/need to continue working but also want more flexibility.*

My friend and colleague Melody McLaren who has helped me better structure my thoughts and arguments for Take Care (as well as for many other projects!), made a conscious decision to quit her job at the responsible business coalition *Business in the Community*, and become a freelance consultant, when she realised her husband, Ian's Parkinson's Disease was getting worse.

*'Consultant is the nice name you put on someone who has to go out in the world and make a living outside of the security of a big organisation', Mel wryly observes.*

*'You have to job-craft — including your caregiving — not with your caregiving on the outside of work'.*

*'You are still multitasking — just to a far greater extent than before!'*

Drawing on her own caring and freelancing journey over the last 10 years, and also listening to the experiences of many other carers-freelancers, Mel gave me her top ten thriving tips.

---

### Melody Mclaren's Thriving Tips For Caring And Freelancing

#### Freelance Working Caregivers: Practical Tips Based on the Business Disability Standard Framework

You are now the CEO of 'You & Co' (as defined by William Bridges, a Consultant/Author who specialised in organisational transitions), an organisation which combines paid work and unpaid caregiving. How can you manage your new hybrid business? A useful framework for thinking about this transition is the Disability Standard developed by the Business Disability Forum.

1. **Commitment**
   - *Decide what your purpose is* — as expressed through your caregiving and your work. What kind of person do you want to be and what are you prepared to do (caring and working) to achieve that goal?

   - *Assess what financial and other resources you will need* for caregiving and working. If you don't have these at present, how can you acquire/develop these over time?

– *Determine who can help you* carry out your dual commitments – family, friends, clients/colleagues, medical/social care professionals.

2. **Know-how**

*Discover how you can become smarter* at combining work and caregiving.

– Are there *networks/communities/friends* or other individuals who face similar challenges and have learned how to manage them?

– Are there *books, websites or other information sources* on the topic of combining work and caregiving from which you can learn and/or get inspired?

– Are there *events* where you can learn more about combining work and caregiving?

– Are there *tax breaks, grants or other financial incentives* that can support your dual working/caregiving activities?

3. **Adjustments**

Determine what sort of adjustments you will need to make to accommodate your caregiving and work responsibilities. These could include:

– *Re-organising your schedule* so that you can provide support for the person you care for – e.g., help with getting up/dressed/fed, accompanying them to medical and other appointments – but also doing your client work, going to meetings, looking after admin.

– If you are currently working in an organisation but intend to transition to self-employment, *seeking support from your line manager, colleagues, HR as well as other professionals (e.g., accountant, solicitor) to make the transition.*

4. Recruitment

Recruit individuals/organisations to your 'support community' who can provide you with backup as a self-employed working caregiver. These can include:

- *Role models*: People you respect who have successfully combined working and caregiving (or working and other demanding roles);

- *Former/current colleagues* who know your strengths and weaknesses and can provide you with honest, practical advice as well as access to resources to support you in your work;

- *Clients* who know and trust you and are prepared to adapt schedules and requirements to accommodate you as a freelance working caregiver;

- *Friends and family* who can provide you with back-up (moral support, advice, respite time/space) as needed;

- *Medical/social care professionals* who are familiar with your circumstances as well as the person you care for and can provide sustainable support over time;

- *Business professionals* such as accountants and solicitors who know your circumstances and can provide you with services to support your business effectively.

5. Retention

To sustain your business, you need to retain the members in your support community but also invest in your own development as a self-employed working caregiver. This means:

> — *Setting aside the time needed to liaise with your support community* to keep them up to date with your circumstances and needs instead of trying to 'go it alone' in difficult times;

> — *Attending to, and cultivating, the skills and knowledge you are developing as a freelance working caregiver* which could be of value to a future client or employer (should you return to organisational employment).

6. **Products and services**

As a self-employed working caregiver, you need to be realistic about what types of work you are able to do in current circumstances. You might wish to consider work-from-home opportunities such as freelance writer, editor, or artist; online tutor; translator; online shop owner or customer service representative.

7. **Suppliers and partners**

Like any other business owner, you need to choose the suppliers and partners with whom you work carefully, particularly as your dual responsibilities require you to function as time- and cost-effectively as possible.

> — Those who provide you with products and services should be aware that because of your dual responsibilities, your requirements for their products and services may emerge at short notice and therefore flexibility will be important to meeting your needs and those of the person(s) you care for. You can work with them to anticipate any scenarios that might arise.

> — Seek advice from trusted members of your support community regarding suppliers who can provide products and services you require;

  - Your business partners need to be made aware
    that your circumstances and availability can change
    at short notice. Therefore, where possible, you
    should work with them to prepare for unexpected
    contingencies.

8. **Communication**

You will need to ensure you communicate effectively with
the different members of your 'support community' as
well as other stakeholders. You can help them (and yourself)
by:

  - Providing clarity as to how (online/phone/face-to-face),
    when (which hours/days) and where (your home/office
    or other location) you can be contacted, given your
    dual responsibilities;

  - Giving individuals a 'heads up,' where possible, when
    you are likely to need their help or your circumstances
    are likely to change.

9. **Premises**

Determine how you need to modify your personal/working
space(s) so that you can effectively support the person you
care for and work. This can mean:

  • If caring for someone with mobility problems, installing
    rails, alternative flooring, making other modifications to
    ensure their safety while simultaneously maintaining as
    much independence for them as possible.

  • If you are working from home, fitting out your home
    office/working space to ensure you have adequate light-
    ing, worktop space, equipment and surroundings to min-
    imise distraction while working.

---

**10. Information and communication technology (ICT)**

Ensure you have the ICT facilities you need to ensure you can work remotely, particularly if you need to accompany the person you care for to appointments outside your home/office. This can include:

- *Investing in a home/office Wi-Fi network* which enables rapid transfer of large files;

- *Investing in a 'mi-fi' device* to tap into 3G/4G networks and create a personal Wi-Fi network to support broadband working on the go.

---

Mel is a naturally organised individual. She has an infectious curiosity and a researcher's terrier-like tenacity to investigate and search out relevant data. She is one of Malcolm Gladwell's 'mavens'. In his best-selling book, 'Tipping Point', about how ideas and movements spread, the American writer Gladwell talks about the critical role of connectors (networkers), sales-people able to communicate and motivate — and mavens. The word maven comes from Hebrew, meaning 'one who understands', based on an accumulation of knowledge: someone who can spot patterns and draw meaning from disparate data. Mel has had more than a decade to deepen her carer knowledge.

Most freelancers won't have Mel's expertise nor necessarily the time or inclination to investigate for themselves. How can other carers who are working freelance and who don't have Mel's maven skills, be helped to ferret out relevant information and resources to make them more resilient both as carers and as freelancers?

One solution would be for caring employers to extend their support to suppliers and especially to their freelance contractors. Another way of supporting carers who are working freelance, would be to extend the kind of umbrella membership of an Employers of Carers network that *Employers for Carers* in the United Kingdom is now piloting, through Small Business Clubs, trade associations and the like: see Part 3 – Chapter 3 page 209 below.

There is also the potential to extend the remit of co-operatives and collectives of self-employed people that are now starting to spring up. These collectives or co-operatives of the self-employed enable freelancers to share costs and services, can take some of the strain out of going it alone. Most use the 'consortia' model, whereby a co-operative provides a range of 'paid for' services to its members who are all self-employed. They, in turn, own and control the company, though they tend to have an essentially flat management structure, with no heads of department and members free to develop and grow the co-operative how they choose.

A 2016 article in The Guardian newspaper notes that 'other countries are further down the road in organising self-help groups. In the United States, the Freelancers Union provides its 280,000 members with advice and insurance. In Belgium, SMart is a co-op offering invoicing and payments for 60,000 freelancer members. In France, new legislation allows self-employed workers to access the sickness pay and benefits of conventional employees through co-operatives'.[145] It is not too fanciful to imagine a few years hence, more joint marketing/admin back-up co-operatives or mutuals of freelancers, also buying into Employee Assistance Programmes providing advise, information and access to emergency back-up care for members juggling their self-employed job and caring.

Whilst co-operatives for the self-employed might, in some cases be able to assist freelancers who are also carers, it really also needs collective action by governments to make information available via their websites and support services for small businesses and the self-employed; and well-resourced public information campaigns to raise awareness that this information is available. In the United Kingdom, the current British Prime Minister, Theresa May, MP has asked the CEO of the RSA Mathew Taylor to look at the situation of the self-employed and I hope he will consider freelancers who are also caring as part of the agenda for his report.

## TAKE-AWAY

Freelancers with caring responsibilities need to take a proactive, holistic approach to their work and caring responsibilities, 'job crafting' a new, coherent identity which encompasses work and caring. Building their own networks of knowledge and people which provide the support they need. These can be enhanced by joining cooperatives of other self-employed carers. Caring employers can also extend their support for employees to contractors with caring responsibilities. Government action is also needed.

# CHAPTER 3

# A SOCIETY THAT CARES: CREATING AN ENABLING ENVIRONMENT FOR MORE EMPLOYERS FOR WORKING CARERS

*Employers are a very important channel to reach carers. Supporting carers to manage work and caring is critical for improving the quality of life of carers; and employers are central to this. The actions or inactions of many different 'actors' can enhance or undermine the efforts of employers. Employers are part of a wider ecosystem of actors who can both themselves better support carers and encourage more employers to take care of working carers. These actors or levers of influence include national governments, regional and local governments and development agencies, employer federations and business representative organisations, skills training agencies, trade unions, associations of human resource (HR) professionals, and independent financial advisers. Better coordination is needed between these actors. A mindset for collaborative commitments ('we could if you would')*

*could transform support for working carers. Individual
citizens also have an important part to play through how
we think about caring, carers and working carers; in our
own behaviours as and to carers; and in the language
we use.*

Much of the passion and the drive to create carer-
friendly workplaces will come from individuals like Helen
Johnson, Emma Bould and Craig Hughes who 'get it' and
do something positive about it. The example of 'early
adopters' like Westpac and Centrica who understand the
business case for being carer-friendly, will gradually infect
other employers. My experience of promoting responsible
business practice, or a better deal for those of us with disabilities or who are gay, all convince me that it is possible
to speed up the adoption process by creating an enabling
environment. There are a range of levers — actors — that
can help create this enabling environment (see **Diagram 1**).

These levers or actors include governments, local/
regional governments and development agencies, skills
training agencies, trade unions and employers/employer
organisations. We need disruptive innovation in technology, public policy, long-term financing, social movements
and cultural values and behaviour to get the most from
these individual actors.

## GOVERNMENTS

Governments have a number of levers at their disposal.
These include legislation, policy-making, convening
power, funding innovation, and what the Americans call

**Diagram 1: Getting more Employers of Carers — Leavers to Influence Change.**

'the bully-pulpit' — the power to exhort and name/fame, name/shame.

Governments can legislate to make carers a protected employment status; to give a statutory right to request flexible working; and to give an entitlement to paid carer leave, as Prof Sue Yeandle explains (page 47 above).

In the 2016 US presidential election campaign, Democratic Party candidate Hillary Clinton, who cared for her elderly mother while serving as secretary of state, proposed spending $10 billion for 10 years to provide tax credits to help offset up to $6,000 in annual caregiving costs for elderly family members, providing credits towards monthly Social Security retirement benefits for caregivers who leave the paid labour force to care for elderly relatives and expanding state-level grants to improve respite care access for family caregivers of children or adults of any age.[146]

Governments can establish a Carers' Strategy to create a vision of and establish a goal for, a society that respects, values and supports carers.

The United Kingdom, Canada, New Zealand and Australia have implemented national strategies that focus on various aspects of supporting caregivers, including: information services, financial support for caregivers, community supports to promote caregivers well-being, legislation to allow for requests for flexible workplace practices, and working with employer organisations to promote the benefits of supporting caregivers in the workplace. At the time of writing, the UK Government is finalising a new cross-government caring strategy for England. (Caring is a devolved responsibility for the other nations of The United Kingdom). This will be the latest iteration of a Caring Strategy. The first was introduced by the Blair Government. The then British Prime Minister spoke movingly of his own experience as a young carer helping his mother look after his father Leo who in later life was paralysed after a stroke. It is anticipated that the new English Carer Strategy will include more support for working carers.

Governments can establish commissions/taskforces to investigate particular aspects of the caring journey or carer needs.

In 2014, the then Government of Canada launched the Canadian Employers for Caregivers Plan (CECP) to explore ways to help employee caregivers participate as fully as possible in the workforce. The CECP was one of a range of activities that the Government of Canada and others undertook to support caregivers. These included tax measures, income replacement through employment insurance, and the provision of targeted programmes for caregivers in populations under federal jurisdiction. One element of the CECP, the Employer Panel for Caregivers.

The Panel was mandated to engage with employers, to identify their best practices for supporting employee caregivers, and share these findings with other Canadian businesses and stakeholders.[147]

Governments can provide tax-breaks for eldercare or other dimensions of caring just as a number of jurisdictions today give tax-breaks for childcare.

## The Belgian Experience

### Policy

A 'service voucher' system was launched in 2004 by the Belgian federal government to encourage the demand and supply of domestic services, with the overall objective of creating employment and improving individuals' work-life balance. This enables people to purchase domestic help from a licensed company and covers services such as cleaning, laundry, ironing, cooking, and transport (for people with low levels of mobility) but excludes personal care. Individuals are able to purchase a voucher for €7.50. Each voucher entitles the user to purchase €21.50

of services from registered service providers. The gap between the cost of the voucher to the user and the value of the services it purchases (€14.00) is funded by the Government.

## Outcomes

164,789 jobs (4.7% of all Belgian jobs) were created between 2004 and 2011 in the domestic services sector alone, corresponding to 96,289 full-time equivalent jobs. Since the inception of this scheme, 2,204 new companies have been established in this sector.

## Costs

The total cost of the scheme was €1.6 billion in 2011, 0.4% of Belgian gross domestic product (GDP). Taking into account the additional tax revenues accruing from the additional economic activity generated by the scheme, the net cost of the scheme has been estimated at between €384 million and €523.3 million p.a.[148]

## The French Experience

### Policy

In 2005, the French government created the 'universal service employment voucher', with the following effects:

> Users can deduct up to 50% of the cost of employing a worker directly, up to €12,000. Users with dependants can deduct up to €15,000. Users with disabilities can deduct 80% of the cost up to a maximum of €20,000.

Organisations providing vouchers to their employees
are entitled to tax credits up to 25% of the total value
of the vouchers provided.

Organisations providing services are exempted from
social security contributions, and benefit from a
reduced value-added tax (VAT) rate of 5.5%.

The scheme aimed to improve individuals' work-life
balance, assist vulnerable groups, and stimulate economic
activity.

## Outcomes

These interventions have created a total of €17.8 billion
in added value in the French economy. 330,000 jobs have
been created since 2005 in a wide range of personal and
household services, including what would be recognised
as care and support in The United Kingdom.

## Costs

The total cost of these interventions in France was
€6.2 billion in 2010 (0.31% of GDP). The total earn-
back effects have been estimated at €9 billion p.a., indicating that the interventions led to the French government
gaining €2.8 billion p.a.[149]

Where there is state provision/support for health-care,
Governments can encourage or mandate their health service explicitly to recognise the role/status of carers who
are often the frontline of a health service.

Carers UK, for example, is seeking a new legal duty on
the National Health Service (NHS) to put in place policies
to identify carers and to promote their health and well-
being – helping to build a carer friendly NHS.

Governments can also fund innovative approaches to identify and support working carers.

## Follow-up Task and Finish Group – Care and Employment Pilots 2015–2017

In 2013, Employers for Carers, Carers UK and the British Government formed a Task and Finish Group to look at how carers could be better supported to remain in work. One of the recommendations from the ensuing landmark report was that Government should look at seed funding innovative projects combining technology and new methods of supporting carers in employment.

As a result, the 2010–2015 Coalition Government launched nine local Carers in Employment pilots exploring ways to help carers balance work with their caring responsibilities. The nine pilot areas explored how technology can be combined with professional support from the Local Authority and the assistance of informal networks of friends, neighbours and Time Bank volunteers to ease the pressure of caring. For example, one pilot will monitor cared for adults by telephone every day at an agreed time, then contact the carer by email or text to confirm that they do not need assistance.

The pilots will also explore how businesses can give employees with caring responsibilities more help, for example, by promoting flexible working patterns and setting up carers 'surgeries'. One pilot will also set up a pop up business school to help carers set up in self-employment.

There are nine pilot sites across the country: North Tyneside; Northamptonshire; Cheshire West; Gateshead; Bury; North Somerset; South Gloucestershire; Staffordshire and Stoke; and Sefton. Pilots run for 2 years 2015–2017.

The Dutch Government funds the national Werk and Mantelzorg project which focuses on encouraging and supporting company initiatives for working carers. It is promoted by Mezzo, a non-governmental organisation (NGO) for caregivers, in cooperation with a HR consulting company.[150]

## LOCAL AND REGIONAL GOVERNMENT AND DEVELOPMENT AGENCIES

Local and regional government can leverage their deep knowledge of community needs and resources, their often powerful role in their local economy, their convening power and sometimes their 'pump-priming' financing to create more of an enabling environment for carers generally and working carers specifically.

In The United Kingdom, several local authorities including Surrey and East and West Sussex County Councils have established local networks of small and medium enterprises (SMEs) who want to improve their help for their employee carers. Several of these local authority-supported SME networks enjoy umbrella membership of Employers for Carers, giving the individual SMEs in their area, access to publications and events.[151] As Sam Tearle from West Sussex Council explains: 'Our vision is that carers should be better able to combine paid employment with their caring role, and/or be able to

return more easily to the job market when their caring
role has ceased.'[152]

## Making London or Any Other City Region or Municipality a Great Place for Carers and Employee Carers

Some of the writing of 'Take Care', coincided with the 4-yearly
election campaign for London Mayor. The 2016 election
produced a new mayor. As a semi-recovered political junkie,
following the twists and turns of the 2016 race, I found myself
wondering what might a Mayor's caring strategy look like?
And in turn, what would be required to make London (or any
other city region or municipality for that matter) a great place
for carers and employee carers?

The Mayor would lead by example, regularly talking about the
role and contribution of caregivers. He or she would detail a
carers' strategy, which would use both statutory powers and
bully-pulpit/convening/influencing roles to develop a joined-up
strategy. The Greater London Authority, and other groups
under the Mayor's control, would have formal policies for their
employee carers as part of their HR and Talent Management
strategy. They would draw on the experience of London organisations like the Transport of London and the Metropolitan
Police, who already have a carers' policy and are proactive in
encouraging staff to identify if they are carers.

Teachers in London schools would be trained and encouraged
to spot pupils who are young carers; and to introduce them to
help for young carers including young carer hubs and services
like the Renaissance Foundation.

GP surgeries would be asking patients if they are a carer or
being cared for; and would encourage carers to visit the

websites of carer organisations for help and advice. GP practices would have adopted carer-inclusive policies.

Business representative organisations would be encouraging their member companies to carer-proof their existing HR policies and establish a carers' policy.

App developers and entrepreneurs in London's Silicon Old Street and neighbouring high-tech hubs would be challenged to develop an App matching those needing quality respite care provision with providers; and other resources to help carers.

There would be a major academic research centre researching, reaching and advising on carers and caring in one of the local universities, that was well-connected to both practice and academic networks around the world, such as the International Centres for Family and Work in Boston College (USA) and at the IESE Business School in Spain.

Local authorities, local enterprise partnerships, health and well-being boards, Business Improvement Districts, Chambers of Commerce and local businesses would be working together to support carers to remain in employment, through adopting flexible work practices, offering carer-leave, peer mentoring and access to high quality advice and information. A Mayoral initiative would match-fund with a leading London entrepreneur, an advice and information service for London's growing army self-employed and small business owners, who are also carers.

The Mayor would also have established a Greater London version of Scotland's 'Carer positive' programme for employers of carers to benchmark their performance on carer-friendly policies and practices.

## TRAINING AND RETRAINING AGENCIES AND
## EMPLOYER LABOUR-MARKET INITIATIVES

State and employer-led training and retraining initiatives can play an important role in helping ex-carers to re-enter the labour market: returnships.

Men and women who gave up work in order to care for a loved one, but whose caring responsibility has ended and who now wish to re-enter the labour market; and to those who have not worked at all because of caring responsibilities.

Giving up work to care can have a negative impact on finances not only for short-term, but also for long-term in terms of reduced pensions pot and savings. There are also other negative impacts such as increased social isolation and ill-health. See Chapter 1.

Many carers will continue to be carers into old age or even to the end of their lives; others will be too old/infirm to start working again by the time their caring has ended. However, there will be a significant minority of ex-carers who are still young enough to want to work again — and who often will need to work. However, as well as the usual challenges facing those out of the formal labour market for prolonged periods, ex-carers are likely to face extra barriers in terms of loss of contacts, out-of-date technical skills and ill-health.

Societies face a major societal time-bomb about funding an extended old age. This will be particularly serious for those who had less/no opportunities to build up any pension pot. It is not only a moral challenge, — but also a very practical problem for society. There is a need to provide customised help to ex-carers just as there has been a business case to help individuals from the BME (Black, Minority and Ethnic) community, living with disabilities, ex-offenders, etc. This is a new frontier for social inclusion.

## TRADE UNIONS

As far back as 1991, the British Trade Union Congress published a Charter for Carers advocating flexible working and a right to return to work for employee carers.

Australian trade unions have been very positive towards carers. The peak body for Australian trade unions the Australian Council of Trade Unions (ACTUs) has enthusiastically advocated for carers for 20 years. Work and care is included in trade union collective agreements negotiated in several European countries including Austria, Germany, Netherlands and Slovenia. In 2014, the European Trade Union Confederation (ETUC) produced a report: 'Who Cares? Experiences and Possibilities to Reconcile Work and Care Responsibilities for Dependent Family Members' to raise the issue of working carers with member federations.

## CREATING NETWORKS OF SUPPORTIVE EMPLOYERS OF CARERS

There are a number of ways that a campaign/initiative to encourage employers to become great employers of carers, could start. The initiative could come from an existing employers federation or business lobby group or a Corporate Responsibility (CR) coalition. Most major economies across the world now have some form of business-led CR Coalition promoting responsible business practices such as Business in the Community in The United Kingdom, Business for Social Responsibility headquartered in California, Corporate Social Responsibility (CSR) in Europe and the National Business Initiative in South Africa. In 'CR Coalitions', my friend and colleague Jane Nelson and I, defined CR Coalitions as:

> *'Independent, non-profit membership organisations that are composed mainly or exclusively of for-profit businesses; that have a board of directors composed predominantly or only of business people; that are core-funded primarily or totally from business; and whose dedicated purpose is to promote responsible business practice'.*[153]

There are also an increasing number of multinational, industry-specific coalitions. Multistakeholder initiatives can be defined as:

> *'Non-profit distributing organisations concerned with corporate responsibility in which businesses are involved but are not predominant in membership, funding and/or governance and accountability'.*

Business representative organisations, employer lobby groups and CR Coalitions can promote the work and care topic in a number of ways such as:

- Include work and care in the coalition's workplace/ responsible employer agenda: The UK coalition Business in the Community has had workplace

campaigns around gender and race for more than
20 years. It has recently started to look at the employee
carer agenda through its existing work on demographic
change and helping employers to prepare better for an
ageing workforce

- Link information and good practice guidance about
  work and care into any existing or planned workplace
  campaigns, for example, on mental health or ageing or
  managing a multigenerational workforce

- Add a work and care category to existing Responsible
  Business Awards

- Incorporate performance on work and caring into their
  CR benchmarking indices as MA'ALA – Israel
  Business for Social Responsibility has done with their
  MA'ALA Index. The criteria that was integrated into
  the Maala index following discussions with Caregivers
  Israel are:

  - Support given to employees that assist in caring for
    a sick family member

  - Access to assistive services given to employees that
    care for a sick family member

The independent committee of experts that sets the
criteria for the Index thought that this is a very important
issue to be address.

- Creating and running a dedicated Carer Positive style
  benchmarking and certification scheme for employers
  of carers

- Establish a network of employers of carers – see
  below.

Why might Business representative organisations, employer lobby groups and coalitions be interested in organising an initiative to encourage employers of carers? Typically, these business-led organisations will be concerned with business impacts in the marketplace, workplace, environment and community/society. Being a responsible employer of carers is integral to the workplace impact area. This will be particularly relevant if a business lobby or coalition has – or is planning – any campaign with member companies around say skills, retaining older workers, health and well-being in the workplace or responding to demographic changes -for the reasons summarised in Part 1 — Chapter 3.

Another approach would be for the initiative to come from a carers' organisation in the way that Carers UK created Employers for Carers.

## WHY SHOULD A CARERS ORGANISATION CONSIDER DEVOTING SCARCE RESOURCES AND ENERGIES TO CREATING AN EMPLOYERS' NETWORK?

There are a number of national associations of and for carers/caregivers. These include:

Carers Denmark — Pårørende i Danmark
Web: www.paaroer.dk

Association Française des Aidants (French Association of carers)
www.aidants.fr

Family Carers Ireland
Web: www.familycarers.ie

Caregivers Israel
http://caregivers.org.il/

Anhörigas Riksförbund (AHR) (Carers Sweden)
Web: www.ahrisverige.se

Carers Australia
Web: www.carersaustralia.com.au

Carers New Zealand
Web: www.carersair.net.nz

National Alliance for Caregiving — USA
Web: www.caregiving.org

Carers Canada
http://www.ccc-ccan.ca/

Carers UK
www.carersuk.org

At the European level, there is Euro-Carers, formed in 2007. Euro-Carers is the European network representing informal carers and their organisations, irrespective of the particular age or health need of the person they are caring for (http://www.eurocarers.org/).

At the international level, there is IACO (International Alliance of Carer Organisations) formed in 2013, after 15 years of informal networking following an international conference in London in 1998.

Many of these organisations and academics specialising in carers and caring, meet in periodic, international caring conferences. The sixth such international conference was held

in Gothenburg, Sweden in September 2015. The seventh
is scheduled for Adelaide Australia in October 2017.[154]

Clearly, the Board and Executive team of a Carers'
organisation would need to consider very carefully before
deciding to allocate scarce resources and energies to trying to create an employers' network. Potential arguments
for doing so include:

— Extra 'channel to market' — to contact carers

— Potential to reach carers at scale and connect with
  many more carers than could reach individually

— Third party (employer) can do the 'heavy lifting' of
  identifying carers

— Addresses a major issue for many carers: successfully
  juggling work and caring

— Can help many more carers to avoid the 'Vicious
  Circle' (see Part 1 — Chapter 1 page 9)

— Can stimulate new, entrepreneurial sources of creativity (employers and employees) to find new solutions to
  the challenges facing working carers such as assistive
  technologies

— Addresses a significant business need for many
  employers (attraction, retention, engagement of
  employees) so can be self-financing/income-generating
  for the carers' organisation.

It may be of course that the carers' organisation does
not yet have relevant employer contacts or the skills to
engage employers, and will need to recruit volunteers and
staff with credibility and expertise to do so. *See Critical
Success Factors below.*

## Where might 'Early Adopter' Employers be Found?

An initial core group of employers might be recruited from:

— Organisations featuring on Great Place to Work or Best Employers rankings

— Businesses with a positive reputation for CR such as Dow Jones Sustainability Index sectoral leaders, Corporate Knights index of the Global 100 most sustainable corporations in the world[155] or local CR benchmarks

— Organisations and organisations with CEOs appearing on Most Admired listings

— Organisations with HR and Talent directors highly ranked by their peers.

The initial group of early adopters can then help to recruit the second wave from amongst their major business customers and suppliers; personal contacts and industry collaborators.

Any campaign might choose to be membership-based — as in the case of Employers for Carers in The United Kingdom or ReACT (Respect A Caregiver's Time) in The United States;[156] or a multistakeholder initiative as in the case of New Zealand's *Employment for Caring* leadership group, whose members include Carers NZ, Business NZ, the NZ Carers Alliance, the NZ Council of Trade Unions, Bupa, the Ministry of Social Development, Work and Income, and the Department of Labour. Employer members include the Waitemata District Health Board.

*Critical Success Factors*

My experience helping to build several CR coalitions and advising other coalitions, and drawing on the experience of successful CR Coalitions around the world, suggests that whatever the precise format of an initiative to employers of carers, there are likely to be a number of Critical Success Factors. These might be summarised as:

— Engaging top leadership of employer members

— Having a critical mass of respected employers with whom non-members would like to be associated

— Capable secretariat with capacity to fashion and deliver an effective work programme; and with the personal presence and skills to engage employers both at senior and operational levels

— Having a realistic but stretching agenda for action for members progressively to implement

— Establishing a vehicle such as a benchmarking index or annual awards for excellence which both stimulate continuous improvement and healthy competition; and also provide an on-going, sustainable source of new marketplace insights and topics for further research and development

— Skill/will to work with leading members on innovation and tackling difficult to solve issues, so that there is a hard business case for leading employers to remain involved

— Developing both hard data and compelling personal stories of individual employee carers/good employers of carers to engage employers and media

— Regular refreshing of the 'ask' of members.

What might be an effective combination of initial activities to fire up a new network of employers of carers? At Business in the Community, we always used to have a campaigning rule: never ask companies to do something without having at least a couple of examples of organisations already doing what you are recommending to others. Similarly, now, at Carers UK, we have another rule: no statistic without an individual story, no individual story without a compelling statistic. A good starting point is to recruit a business leader who can champion the initiative with his or her peers. They will need a compelling 'ask' – an *Agenda for Action* to pitch. The first recruits are always the hardest to obtain. It helps if these early adopters are well-respected, successful organisations that others will want to listen to and team up with.

Once there is a critical mass of employers, ready and willing to share their experiences, learn from each other and encourage others, it becomes easier to host networking events, produce good practice guides and start raising the bar of performance. Award schemes can be an effective way of generating case studies to promote to others.

I was recently in Israel speaking to separate MA'ALA and Caregivers Israel events. Major Israeli NGOs concerned with ageing have recognised the growing importance of the caring agenda and the need for more support for carers. Caregivers Israel has some seedcorn funding to recruit some employers interested in work and caring. Simultaneously, MA'ALA has recognised the growing importance of caring and ageing as part of what it means to be an inclusive and responsible employer. MA'ALA has secured 2-year funding from the Government to research the 'ageing well' topic, scan international

experience and practice and develop an agenda for action
for Israeli employers.

There is obviously an opportunity to find the synergies
and opportunities for collaboration. This might include,
for example, adding ageing well and caring to the CSR
Manager Training programme run annually by MA'ALA;
organising joint workshops for HR and CSR directors;
and identifying emergent practice from the responses on
caring in the 2017 MA'ALA Index. Working together,
MA'ALA and Caregivers Israel have an exciting opportunity to build a critical mass of Israel-based employers
caring for their carers.

## PROFESSIONAL ASSOCIATIONS FOR HUMAN RESOURCES MANAGEMENT

Both the CIPD (Chartered Institute for Personnel
Development) based in The United Kingdom and the
Society for HR Management in The United States, have
addressed the issue of caring and working. The CIPD, for
example, published a valuable Policy Report in May
2016: 'Creating longer, more fulfilling working lives:
Employer practice in five European countries', which
included sections on helping older workers with their caring responsibilities. There is an opportunity to raise the
topic of caring and working higher up the agenda of
other HR professional associations, for example, through
the annual congress of the European Association of
People Management. Caring for working carers should
certainly be part of research and teaching of International
HR Management professionals in business schools.

## INDEPENDENT FINANCIAL ADVISERS

For many self-employed and small business owner-managers who are also carers, in particular, a further potential lever could be through their Independent Financial Advisers (IFAs). Forward-thinking IFAs will already be asking many more questions during client review meetings regarding future care planning for clients and their ageing parents, starting with the critical importance of up to date Wills and Power of Attorney (Financial, Health and Welfare) and considerations in assisted living/care provision. This includes the challenges of getting/choosing good care, be it funded by government or personally and also the difficulties finding really good care homes. Clearly knowing what benefits are available and how they are claimed is an important part of this. There is a CPD (Continuing Professional Development) programme for all advisers although the level to which they study Care and related subjects is very much down to their own design and learning goals and objectives.

There is a Long-term Care examination that covers care provision. Unsurprisingly, the syllabus appears to be very focused on the financials. Good IFA's would build this into pre- and post-retirement planning as part of cash flow modelling to help clients understand their options. Clearly the financials are vital but equally important is for advisers to understand the emotional stress and day-to-day reality that is dealing with someone in need of care, for example, suffering from dementia.

As Calum Cameron, an experienced Professional Financial Planner comments: 'my guess is there is a long way to go to get the appropriate level of awareness needed in this key area'. Cameron suggests an on line 'client journey' and resource centre that would help people understand the options available and give a step by step guide to simplify the process.

One such resource centre is SOLLA (Society of Later Life Advisers): The SOLLA which was founded in The United Kingdom in 2008 as a not-for-profit organisation, to 'meet the need of consumers, advisers and those who provide financial products and services to the later life market'. SOLLA's aim is to 'ensure that people are better informed about the financial issues of later life and can find a fully accredited adviser quickly and easily'. SOLLA does this through raising the standards of practice of those engaged in advising in older people by promoting the highest levels of professionalism in financial advice through a rigorous accreditation process; identifying and developing best practice by provision of high-quality training and the distribution of the latest information and know how in later life issues; and acting as a source of technical excellence for their 420 Later Life Advisers.[157]

## COLLABORATIVE COMMITMENTS

In Part 3 — Chapter 1, I quoted a Pyramid of carer needs developed by Prof Janet Fast in Canada. We could speculate about how addressing these needs could be accelerated if different actors: governments, employers, carers associations, service charities, health providers, etc. could develop their work and programmes with reference to each other. Even better if these different actors deliberately designed their own interventions so as to encourage others to bring forward/expand their own contributions. Elsewhere, this has been described as the process of 'collaborative commitments'.

'Collaborative commitments' are agreements made voluntarily between individuals and organisations from business, public sector and civil society, to achieve positive social impacts which would not be possible for one sector acting alone, to obtain.[158]

The concept of Collaborative Commitments was inspired by the practical example of the International Finance Facility for Immunisation (IFFIm). Through the IFFIm, the private sector created a financial mechanism (the bond) to enable the public sector to front-load the release of its resource (funding for international development) to the third sector who delivered the intervention (in this case childhood immunisation). The key is that each partner used its own unique contribution to release the potential of another – and that without any one of the key collaborators, the commitment would fail, and the positive impacts (more healthy people whose lives are not destroyed or stunted by preventable diseases) would not have materialised. In this case, financiers recognised that commercial markets could be harnessed to provide accelerated cash flows for mass, child immunisation in developing countries, based on the guarantees of participating national governments of their future funding streams for development. Crucially, however, it was also recognised that having more money available earlier would be a necessary but insufficient requirement without the means of ensuring that the money could be well spent, on the ground, through NGOs able to rise to the challenge of increasing their own capacity to deliver the immunisation programme. Key to the success of this collaborative commitment were, therefore, the bankers able to design and market the commercial bond in the international markets (Goldman Sachs); the national finance ministers and their governments (Italy, Spain, The United Kingdom, etc.) who committed to forward projections of development funding that would be made available for immunisation, on which the commercial bond was guaranteed; and the NGOs through which the increased capacity for immunisation would be delivered through The Global Alliance for Vaccines and Immunization (GAVI).

In turn, the experience of GAVI on the ground encouraged others such as the Gates Foundation – which now has an annual budget twice that of the World Health Organisation – to develop the capacity of frontline organisations on the ground. Hence, this 'collaborative commitment' led to a chain reaction.

How might this concept of Collaborative Commitments apply to employee-carers?

If employers offer flexible work and carer leave, a *quid pro quo* Collaborative Commitment might be government investing in technology R&D (Rural and Development), for example, in The United Kingdom through the Technology Strategy Board now called Innovate UK, to improve the quality and extent of second tier of the pyramid, that is, services for users and carers.

In Australia, Apple, Microsoft and other technology companies have said they will trial adaptive technologies explicitly because of the Australian National Disability Insurance Scheme (NDIS).[159]

Another potential example of a Collaborative Commitment, might be a group of employers willing to commit to offer subsidised respite care (perhaps as one of the available employee benefits in a cafeteria of benefits that individual employees can pick and choose from, to a specified annual value); in return for Government giving tax incentives/start-up subsidies for small businesses/ social enterprises offering respite care. This might draw on the experience of the French and Belgian market-making schemes described above page 205.

Collaborative Commitments also need to include individual citizens — both as carers and potentially also as someone being cared for, for example, in terms of accessible housing.

## TAKE-AWAY

To create an enabling environment for developing more carer-friendly workplaces and societies, enlightened employers can engage in collaborative commitments with carer associations, CR coalitions, governments, local and regional government and development agencies, health services, academic institutions, chambers of commerce, trade unions and other actors to raise awareness and implementation of best practices in carer support.

# TAKE CARE — CONCLUSION

No one should have to care alone. I passionately believe that we can and must end carer isolation. It will be good for carers themselves, for the loved ones they are caring for, and for the rest of society.

Just how far we still have to travel in recognising and honouring caring as one of the life stages, came home to me in a recent conversation I had with a leading female business figure. It was quickly clear to me that she had neither comprehension nor empathy for the choices I happily made in reducing work to care for my mother. My hope is that her view increasingly represents the past; and that a new generation of leaders will be more inclusive and enlightened, and see caring as a natural life stage to be embraced and reconciled with work.

As we saw in Part 1, Chapter 1, several carers associations around the world have calculated the replacement costs to the state if the voluntary caring contribution of carers had to be replaced. An August 2015 Deloitte Australia study for Caregivers Australia, for example, suggests that in Australia at least, the propensity to care has actually decreased. Research in the United Kingdom suggests that the United Kingdom might see a tipping point between the number of those needing care and available carers in 2017. Whilst China has now relaxed its one-child policy introduced in 1979, the effects will be felt for decades to come as China experiences the most rapid and dramatic ageing of any population anywhere ever. One child could be caring in future for two parents and four grandparents.

It is both morally right and bottom-line common-sense to help carers to be as effective and as personally resilient as possible. It is particularly sensible to help those of us who are in work and can/want to continue working whilst caring, to do so.

The examples quoted in Take Care emphasise that there is not a 'one-size fits all' policy for employers of carers. There is, however, plenty of emerging practice for the kinds of things that employers can do — both from examples of specific caring policies and practices; but also by extension from successful practices in other aspects of Human Resources such as supporting employees with disabilities, or flexible working.

Organisations will have to decide: through negligence/indifference are we going to compound our talent pipeline challenges; do we want to ensure employee carers can *survive* in work — or make it possible that they can *thrive*? For employee carers to thrive at work, is going to require a mindset shift: from carers themselves as well as from employers and wider society.

In the coming decade, I hope that many more countries will follow the example of the pioneering countries for supporting carers listed in Part 3, Chapter 3, and create carers' alliances. I see an analogy with the way that business coalitions promoting Corporate Responsibility spread in the decade after 1992 from a handful of countries — as my friend and colleague Jane Nelson and I chronicled in our book 'Corporate Responsibility Coalitions: The Past, Present and Future of alliances for Sustainable Capitalism'. I further hope that many of these new putative carers associations will make the creation of an employers network like *Employers for Carers* in the United Kingdom or *ReACT* in the United States, an early priority. As I discussed in Part 3, Chapter 3, such networks of employers of carers might equally be initiated by a business representative organisation, a Corporate Responsibility coalition — or indeed by a government. Whoever initiates a network of employers of carers, and whatever form it takes (an employers network or a multi-stakeholder initiative as in New Zealand), the good news is that there will be some earlier role models — not to slavishly copy but to learn from and build on. As an instinctive campaigner, I can envisage new networks of employers of carers targeting those employers which:

– have their own structured employee networks already, for example, for gender, faith groups, LGBT, disabilities, BME etc.;

– have publicly committed to responsible business practices and/or Great Place to Work or equivalent workplace rankings.

Sharing good practice, encouraging friendly competition for continuous improvement and using the endorsement of existing employers of carers to draw in other employers, means that new networks of employers of carers should be able to get many more organisations engaged faster and more effectively than relying on organic growth. I also passionately believe that we can learn from other successful campaigns to engage employers.

## OPEN FOR BUSINESS

As I was writing *Take Care*, I observed with great admiration and no small envy, the launch of a campaign targeted at employers internationally called Open for Business.

Open For Business is a response by a number of leading global businesses to the spread of anti-LGBT sentiment in many parts of the world.

These businesses share a deep-rooted commitment to diversity and inclusion in their own workplaces, and they are concerned about the growth of anti-LGB&T policies in many countries in which they operate. The Open For Business coalition was launched at the Clinton Global Initiative Annual Meeting in New York on the 29th September 2015.

Open for Business is the brainchild of Jon Miller, a partner at the International Corporate Communications Agency Brunswick. I first met Jon when he was finalising with his co-author Lucy Parker, an excellent book about the impact of responsible business called 'Everybody's Business: The unlikely story of how big business can fix the World (Biteback 2013)'. Jon and Lucy were 'borrowing' the title of my first book: 'Everybody's Business: Managing Risks and Opportunities in Today's Global Society' and with impeccable good manners, they wanted to check that my co-author Adrian Hodges and I did not mind their appropriation of our title. Inspired by what he had learnt about the power of responsible business, Jon wanted to see if it would be possible to galvanise a critical mass of global employers to come out on LGBT rights at work.

With the support of Brunswick, he marshalled a compelling, bottom-line business case for employers thus demonstrating my belief that the case for responsible business should always be hard-headed rather than soft-hearted. Working through the Brunswick client network, Miller assembled an A-list of global employers as initial supporters.

These included: Accenture, American Express, Barclays, Google, IBM, LinkedIn, Mastercard, McKinsey & Company, Microsoft, Standard Chartered, Thomson Reuters and Virgin.

An early target was the annual Davos meeting of the influential World Economic Forum where the global elite debate mega trends, sustainable development and international relations. Miller and his colleagues persuaded the World Economic Forum to run a series of blogs on LGBT rights in the run-up to the 2016 meeting and to include sessions on Open for Business in Davos.

As *The Economist* has noted:

> *Last year {2016}, there appeared to have been a breakthrough of sorts. As well as the usual fringe meeting – this time moderated by Zanny Minton Beddoes, The Economist's editor-in-chief – there was a pep talk from Joe Biden, America's vice president. And, most significantly of all for Davos regulars, a discussion of LGBT issues actually*

*made it onto the official agenda, albeit held in the back room of a Davos hotel, not in the Congress Centre, where the really important conversations take place. This drew a high-powered crowd, including the prime minister of Luxembourg, the Canadian treasury secretary, both gay men, and the bisexual female chief executive of Lloyd's of London, and encouraging words from one of Africa's leading politicians, Ngozi Okonjo-Iweala.*

*This year, even more prominence is expected to be given to LGBT issues, which may finally make it into the Congress Centre itself. There will be a panel discussion on the business case for LGBT diversity and inclusion, and another panel looking at gender identity from a scientific perspective (including highlighting issues around unconscious biases, gender preferences and sexual orientation)'.*[160]

Building on the momentum with global media and opinion-leaders, Open for Business and its supporting employers has followed up with round tables in a number of countries where LGBT rights are most threatened such as Uganda.

It is early days for Open for Business but already it is possible to discern a number of critical success factors that they have enjoyed:

- An international constituency of influential and well-networked professionals, committed to human rights and diversity and willing to lobby their own organisations and to harness their networks to drive change;

- A core group of committed and well-connected individuals able to commit time and resources to provide a focal point: 'a secretariat';

- Access to sophisticated media and social media skills to fashion and promote the core arguments;

- Top-level 'buy-in' and support from a group of high profile and credible global employers, willing to lend their organisational reputation and weight to the campaign;

- The right kind of personal connections to get Open for Business onto well-established and influential, high-profile existing platforms such as the Clinton Global Initiative and the World Economic Forum.

Just before Davos 2017, Miller told me: 'The programme continues to grow, slowly but surely — we are rolling out events in challenging countries, and we have a couple of interesting things planned for Davos this year. It continues to be a difficult conversation to have in many parts of the world, but we are keeping on'.[161]

Ten or 20 years ago, Open for Business would not have got anything like the traction that it has been able to attract today. As The Economist newspaper noted in a 2014 cover-story on LGBT rights:

> The change in attitudes to homosexuality in many countries — not just the West but also Latin America, China and other places — is one of the wonders of the world. (Human rights: The gay divide; Victories for gay rights in some parts of the world have provoked a backlash elsewhere — 11 October 2014)

I personally have benefitted from the greater tolerance and recognition of LGBT rights. Naturally, therefore, I am an enthusiastic supporter of campaigns like Open for Business. It is not, therefore, to detract or question initiatives like Open for Business, however, to reflect that caring affects even more people, so how can we emulate campaigns like Open for Business, for working carers?

## A CALL TO ACTION

I would like to think that as well as being a how-to guide, Take Care is an extended manifesto, a call to action, that might catalyse one or more of groups such as the Elders, the B Team, the World Economic Forum, Business for Social Responsibility or the International Chamber of Commerce to champion work and caring. Additionally there are now several relatively youthful 'elder statesmen' such as Barack Obama or David Cameron who could themselves galvanise international attention on working carers, if they so chose. I have tried to show, however, that the initiative to trigger an organisation to start caring for its carers, can start with anyone. Having a particular job title or a particular degree of seniority or even any prior knowledge of help for carers, are not essential. Any of us, if sufficiently motivated and persistent can start the ball rolling. At Cranfield University, for example, having had a long conversation with the University's HR director at the beginning of 2016, I sent her periodic inquiries and forwarded useful materials throughout the year. Now the University is consulting with employees, trade unions and managers on the content of a carers policy, which will be launched during 2017.

## A PARADIGM OR EQUILIBRIUM SHIFT

We need what Thomas Kuhn described as a paradigm shift — or as the Skoll Foundation now prefers — an equilibrium shift.[162] With smart phones, social media, intense global connectivity — as chronicled by Joshua Ramo Cooper in the Seventh Sense (2016), it is now possible to dream of ending carer isolation — and building communities (including work communities) that respect, value and support carers.

I am a great believer in not re-inventing the wheel. Many organisations already have built up a lot of practical experience in supporting communities of identity in their workforce such as disabled, BME or LGBT employees. Similarly, many organisations in recent years have committed to Corporate Responsibility and Sustainability. Whilst supporting working carers makes sense on its own merits, it can also be seen as part of a bigger picture of engaging employees and being a responsible organisation — and learning, therefore, can be read across. As someone who has worked for several decades promoting corporate responsibility and sustainability, and advocating for human rights of disabled and older people, I am naturally looking at the synergies and the transferable learning between these fields. There are also important synergies to be developed with leading employers now championing 'agile' workplaces.[163]

I have a vision of employers' policies and practices being supportive and flexible for working carers; that professional care services are sufficiently accessible, reliable and affordable; and that smart technologies are sufficiently innovative and customer-friendly that it is possible for many, many more employees to stay in work, continue to enjoy life — and be better carers too. Hopelessly idealistic? Impossible? Well I remember the wise words of Nelson Mandela: 'It always seems impossible until it's done'.

This is not an issue for 2027 or 2037 — we face the fear urgency of now. If you are an employer of carers, I hope you will take up the challenge of making your workplace a 'champion' — for the benefit of your caring colleagues as well as your organisation as a whole, regardless of size.

It is a formidable task — but as my inspirational mum often used to tell me — if you don't start a task, you will never know just what can be achieved!

# END-NOTES

[1]Johnnie and Tiggy Walker are patrons of Carers UK. Tiggy's account of her journey as carer and then being cared for, is movingly described in her book Unplanned Journey, 2015.

[2]http://www.theguardian.com/guardian-observer-style-guide-c

[3]*Supporting Carers in Your Workforce: A Manager's Handbook.* Employers for Carers; 2015.

[4]Data collected by Carers UK.

[5]http://www.age-platform.eu/age-work/age-policy-work/health/age-work/2656-interactive-platform-for-informal-carers-launched

[6]*Summary – Unpaid help: who does what?* – SCP.

[7]Caregiving in the United States, National Alliance for Caregiving in collaboration with AARP (2009, November).

[8]Australian Bureau of Statistics (ABS). (2015). Retrieved from https://www.yooralla.com.au/news-and-media/statistics-and-infographics/support-carers,-family-and-support-workers/carers-in-australia. Accessed in October 2015.

[9]Cranswick, K. (1997). *Canada's caregivers: Canadian social trends*. Ottawa: Statistics Canada.

[10]Sinha, M. (2012). *Portrait of caregivers* (Catalogue number 89-652-X). Retrieved from http://www.statcan. gc.ca/pub/89-652-x/89-652-x2013001-eng.pdf. Accessed in September 2013.

[11]2012 General Social Survey (GSS). Canada, 2012.

[12]Creating longer, more fulfilling working lives: employer practice in five European countries, CIPD May 2016.

[13]https://sustainabledevelopment.un.org/?menu=1300

[14]Carers UK. (2015). State of Caring Report 2015.

[15]Alone and Caring. (2015). Retrieved from http://www. carersuk.org/for-professionals/policy/policy-library/alone-caring. Accessed in April 2017.

[16]http://news.gc.ca/web/article-en.do?nid=923149

[17]Goyer A. (2015). *Juggling life, work and caregiving.*

[18]Resnizky, S., Cohen, Y., & Brodsky J. (2016, December). *Family caregivers and working life.* Myers-JDC-Brookdale Institute Center for Research on Aging.

[19]Work + Care: Information for Employers. Retrieved from http://www.carers.net.nz/work-care-information-employers

[20]Hollander, J. M., Liu, G., & Chappell, N. (2009). Who cares and how much. *Healthcare Quarterly, 12*(2), 42–49.

[21]Canadian Institute for Health Information. (2012). *National Health Expenditure Trends, 1975 to 2012,*

*Table A1, $182 billion Total Health Expenditures in 2009.*

[22]https://caregiver.org/selected-caregiver-statistics

[23]http://www.aarp.org/content/dam/aarp/ppi/2015/valuing-the-invaluable-2015-update-undeniable-progress.pdf

[24]Reinhard, S. C., Feinberg, L. F., Choula, R., & Houser, A. *Insight on the issues valuing the invaluable: 2015 update.* AARP Public Policy Institute.

[25]Deloitte Access Economics 2015.

[26]http://www.carers.net.nz/blog/economic-value-and-impacts-family-caregiving-new-zealand-0

[27]Buckner, L. (2015). *Valuing Carers 2015.* University of Leeds & Sue Yeandle, University of Sheffield.

[28]Her Majesty's Treasury Public Expenditure Statistical Analyses 2015.

[29]Forbes, www.forbes.com/companies/hsbc-holdings; www.forbes.com/companies/visa quoted in Valuing Carers 2015: The rising value of carers' support.

[30]Buckner, L. (2015). *Valuing Carers 2015.* University of Leeds & Sue Yeandle, University of Sheffield.

[31]*Speaking to 6th International Caring Conference,* Gothenburg, Sweden, September 2015.

[32] Stages of the Caring Journey — Emily Holzhausen — September 2016, Carers UK internal working paper.

[33]Based on meeting 25 November 2016 and subsequent e-mail exchange.

[34]Carers UK. (2015). *State of Caring 2015,* Carers UK.

[35]http://www.caringacross.org/stories/why-working-care-givers-need-paid-leave/

[36]http://www.caringacross.org/stories/caregiving-while-working-full-time/

[37]https://www.amazon.com/Alzheimers-Through-My-Mothers-Eyes-ebook/dp/B00H5QAY3A

[38]Based on: Inspiration – Carers Canada. Work & Care A Balancing Act p. 17 (2015); author's interview 18 July 2016; and subsequent email exchange 2016-2017

[39]Carers UK Caring magazine 2016; interview with author 16 January 2017 and e-mail exchange

[40]Text provided by Vivien Kwok and subsequent emails 2016-2017.

[41]http://www.recruitment-international.co.uk/news/employers-need-to-do-more-to-help-carers-27033.htm

[42]Quoted in The Financial Times The Big Read: US board composition: male, stale and frail? By Stephen Foley and Jennifer Bissell and David Oakley Published 16 August 2016.

[43]https://www.sa.gov.au/topics/community-support/carers/carers-and-employment/for-employers-of-carers

[44]Yeandle S., Caring for our carers: An international per-spective on policy developments in the UK, IPPR blog August 2016 http://www.ippr.org/juncture/caring-for-our-carers

[45]*Ibid.*

[46]Metlife Mature Market Institute, National Alliance for Caregiving. (2006). *The MetLife caregiving cost study:*

*productivity losses to U.S. Business.* Retrieved from http://www.caregiving.org/data/Caregiver%20Cost%20Study.pdf

[47]Duxbury, L., Higgins, C., & Schroeder, B. (2009). Balancing paid work and caregiving responsibilities: A closer look at family caregivers in Canada. A report submitted to Human Resources and Skills Development Canada. Retrieved from http://www.cprn.org/documents/51061_EN.pdf. Accessed on April 2017.

[48]Sherman, K.C., & Reed, K. (2008). Eldercare and job productivity: An accommodation analysis. *Journal of Leadership Studies, 1*(4), 23–36.

[49]Quoted in Government of Canada. (2015 January 21). When work and caregiving collide: How employers can support their employees who are caregivers. Report from the Employer Panel for Caregivers. Retrieved from http://www.ehospice.com/canadaenglish/Default/tabid/10678/ArticleId/13740. Accessed on April 2017.

[50]Lilly, M.B., Laporte, A., & Coyte, P. (2007). Labor market work and home care's unpaid caregivers: A systematic review of labor force participation rates, predictors of labor market withdrawal, and hours of work. *The Milbank Quarterly, 85*, 641–690.

[51]Lilly, M. (2010). Curtailing the cost of caring for employers and employees: What every CEO should know, Von Canada.

[52]Hegewisch, A. (2009). Flexible working policies: A comparative review. Research Report 16. Equality and Human Rights Commission. Manchester: Equality and Human Rights Commission.

[53]Quoted in Slaughter, A.-M. (2015). Unfinished Business. p. 229.

[54]http://www.100yearlife.com/

[55]Business in the Community. (2015). The Missing Million.

[56]Kumar, V., & Pansari, A. (2015). Measuring the benefits of employee engagement. *MIT Sloan Management Review, 56*(4), 67–72.

[57]Shuck, B., & Reio, T. G. (2014). Employee engagement and well-being: A moderation model and implications for practice. *Journal of Leadership and Organizational Studies, 21*(1), 43–58.

[58]Kruse, K. (2015). The ROI of employee engagement. *Health Care Registration: The Newsletter For Health Care Registration Professionals, 24*(6), 3–5.

[59]Lightle, S. S., Castellano, J., Baker, B., & Sweeney, R. J. (2015). The role of corporate boards in employee engagement. *IUP Journal of Corporate Governance, 14*(4), 7–13.

[60]Lifeng, Z., Wayne, S. J., & Liden, R. C. (2016). Job engagement, perceived organizational support, high-performance human resource practices, and cultural value orientations: A cross-level investigation. *Journal of Organizational Behavior, 37*(6), 823–844.

[61]Sivarethinamohan, R., & Aranganathan, P. (2011). Determinants of employee engagement and retention practices in indian corporate-principal component analysis. *Asia Pacific Journal of Research in Business Management, 2*(12), 1–17.

[62]Downey, S. N., Werff, L., Thomas, K. M., & Plaut, V. C. (2015). The role of diversity practices and inclusion in promoting trust and employee engagement. *Journal of Applied Social Psychology*, 45(1), 35–44. doi:10.1111/jasp.12273

[63]Benito-Osorio, D., Muñoz-Aguado, L., & Villar, C. (2014). The Impact of Family and Work-Life Balance Policies on the Performance of Spanish Listed Companies. *M@N@GEMENT*, 17(4), 214–236.

[64]Gastfriend, J. (2014). No one should have to choose between caregiving and work, Harvard Business Review Blog. Retrieved from https://hbr.org/2014/07/no-one-should-have-to-choose-between-caregiving-and-work/. Accessed on July 23, 2014.

[65]Downey, S. N., Werff, L., Thomas, K. M., & Plaut, V. C. (2015). The role of diversity practices and inclusion in promoting trust and employee engagement. *Journal of Applied Social Psychology*, 45(1), 35–44. doi:10.1111/jasp.12273

[66]Vogel, N. (2006). Meeting special needs: A benefit that adds value for both employees and employers. *Compensation and Benefits Review*, 38(2), 57–61. doi:10.1177/0886368706287370

[67]Shankar, T., & Bhatnagar, J. (2010). Work Life Balance, Employee Engagement, Emotional Consonance/Dissonance & Turnover Intention. Indian Journal Of Industrial Relations, 46(1), 74–87.

[68]Ali Omran, S. K. (2016). Work-family balance dilemma among employed parents (An empirical study).

*International Journal of Business and Economic Development,* 4(1), 31–46.

[69]Rothmann, S., & Baumann, C. (2014). Employee engagement: The effects of work-home/home-work interaction and psychological conditions. *South African Journal of Economic and Management Sciences, 17*(4), 515–530.

[70]Boyar, S. L., Wagner, T. A., Petzinger, A., & McKinley, R. B. (2016). The impact of family roles on employee's attitudes and behaviors. *Journal of Management Development, 35*(5), 623–635. doi:10.1108/JMD-07-2015-0096

[71]Shankar, T., & Bhatnagar, J. (2010). Work life balance, employee engagement, emotional consonance/dissonance and turnover intention. *Indian Journal of Industrial Relations, 46*(1), 74–87.

[72]Christ, G. (2016). Kicking wellness out of the workplace. *EHS Today, 9*(4), 15–17.

[73]http://www.cipd.co.uk/pressoffice/press-releases/cipd-absence-management-061014.aspx

[74] Author interview.

[75]Author interview with Sharon Graff and subsequent e-mail exchanges.

[76]Blueprint for Better Business. Retrieved from http://www.blueprintforbusiness.org/

[77]Employer Resource Guide Four Steps For Supporting Employees With Caregiving Responsibilities – ReACT.

[78]Best practice in supporting carers, Carer Positive Scotland, 2016.

[79]Quoted in Presentation to Sixth International Caring conference, Gothenburg, Sweden, September 2015.

[80]Snelling, S. (2014, March 26). *Caregiving is a corporate issue: Next avenue.* Retrieved from http://www.nextavenue.org/caregiving-corporate-issue/

[81]Carers NSW 2014 Carer Survey.

[82]Presentation to Sixth International Caring Conference, Gothenburg, Sweden, 3–6 September 2015.

[83]MetLife Mature Market Institute, & National Alliance for Caregiving. (2003). The MetLife Study of Sons at Work. Retrieved from www.caregiving.org

[84]Source: Euro-carers. *European association working for carers, We care – Do you? Balancing work and care – An employer's guide* (p. 8).

[85]ReACT Employer resources: http://www.aarp.org/react/info-09-2013/react-johnshopkins-case-study.html

[86]Speech at 6th International Carers Conference, Gothenburg, 4 September 2015 as recorded by author.

[87]Anne-Marie Slaughter. Unfinished Business. p. 207.

[88]ReACT Employer resources. Retrieved from http://www.aarp.org/react/info-09-2013/react-johnsonjohnson-case-study.html

[89]Speech at 6th International Carers Conference, Gothenburg, 4 September 4 2015 as recorded by author.

[90] Based on interview on 7 October 2015, further meeting on 19 October 2016 and e-mail exchanges 2016–2017.

[91] Sourced from Melville-Ross, J., Two for Joy 2016; various newspaper articles at the time of book publication; Melville-Ross article for International Business Times; and author interview on 20 January 2017.

[92] Interview with Tim Fallowfield, 24 August 2016.

[93] Based on published sources and see the TED talk with Steve Shirley filmed March 2015 (http://www.steveshirley.com/about/)

[94] Collins & Porras, Built to Last, 1994.

[95] http://www.bitcni.org.uk/news/business-in-the-community-launches-employee-passport/

[96] Work & Care: The Necessary Investment: Combining Work and Care, The business case for carer-friendly workplaces -Report No. 2 Work & Care Initiative, Carers Australia, 2014.

[97] Quoted in Brufal, T. (December 2016). If you were a carer, what support would your organisation offer you? Forward Institute.

[98] Kumar, V., & Pansari, A. (2015). Measuring the benefits of employee engagement. MIT Sloan Management Review, 56(4), 67–72. http://www.topemployersforworkingfamilies.org.uk/index.php/special-awards/case/west-dunbartonshire-council

[99] http://www.mitsubishicorp.com/jp/en/about/resource/diversity.html

[100]http://www.mitsubishicorp.com/jp/en/about/resource/diversity.html

[101]Interview with Neville Hounsome Group, HR Director and Sarah Bissell Head of Reward, Hyde Housing, 21 March 2016.

[102]Bowness, S. (2015, August 18). *The future of work: Why employers are caring for the caregivers*, The Globe and Mail, August 18, 2015.

[103]See more at: http://www.shrm.org/hrdisciplines/benefits/articles/pages/2012nse.aspx#sthash.PhjTmJRg.dpuf

[104]Schurman, B. (2016). OECD Business Brief: Who cares for the caregivers. Retrieved from http://www.oecd.org/forum/oecdyearbook/who-cares-for-the-carevigers.htm

[105]Based on author interview and e-mail exchanges with Westpac 2016–2017.

[106]Derived from published sources and from their website: http://otsuka.csrportal.jp/en

[107]http://eurocarers.org/InformCare

[108]http://solutions.3m.com/wps/portal/3M/en_US/healthy-living/home/family/adult-elder-care/

[109]http://hr.harvard.edu/caring-elders-and-other-adults

[110]http://www.workingmums.co.uk/top-employers/unilever/

[111]Snelling, S. (2015, April 14). *A New Era: Companies Supporting Caregivers, Forbes, Next Avenue*. Retrieved from http://www.forbes.com/sites/nextavenue/

2015/04/14/a-new-era-companies-supporting-caregivers/
#10a9c1c20de4. Accessed on April 14, 2015.

[112]http://www.taisei.co.jp/english/index.html

[113]Quoted in http://www.aarp.org/react/react-employer-best-practices/

[114]Author interview with Frank Nigriello 19 July 2016
and subsequent e-mail exchange 2016–2017.

[115]Quoted in Brufal T, 'If you were a carer, what support
would your organisation offer you?' Forward Institute,
December 2016.

[116]Author interviews with Susan Scott-Parker on 4
February 2016 and 18 January 2017 and e-mail
exchanges 2016–2017.

[117]Age UK, & Carers UK. (July 2016). *Walking the tight-rope: The challenges of combining work and care in later life.*

[118]Presentation, Carer Positive, Glasgow, February 2016.

[119]Author interview.

[120]Nash N. (2009). *Disabled employee networks: A prac-tical guide.* Kate Nash Associates.

[121]Interview with Keith Edwards April 2015 and subse-quent e-mail exchanges.

[122]Presentation to Employers for Carers Networking
event October 2016 and e-mail exchanges 2016.

[123]*Disabled Employee Networks: A practical guide.*, Kate
Nash Associates. 2015.

[124]Quoted in Brufal, T., (December 2016). 'If you were a carer, what support would your organisation offer you?' Forward Institute.

[125]Author e-mail exchange August 2015.

[126]http://www.carerpositive.org/

[127]Author interview on 31 July 2015 and follow-up e-mail exchange January 2017.

[128]Carers UK case-study.

[129]http://www.responsible100.com/

[130]See more at: http://www.aarpinternational.org/ resource-library/resources/grosser-cleaning-and-care-services-2014-aarp-best-employer-international-award-recipient#sthash.O6mxdPn2.dpuf

[131]Author interview January 2017.

[132]Gratton, L., & Scott, A. (2016). *The 100 year life.* Bloomsbury Information.

[133]EU Commission Communication on CSR (October 2011). Retrieved from http://ec.europa.eu/enterprise/policies/sustainable-business/files/csr/new-csr/act_en.pdf. Accessed on April 2017.

[134]Ainsbury, R., & Grayson, D. (2014). Business critical: Understanding a company's current and desired stages of corporate responsibility maturity, Doughty Centre for Corporate Responsibility Occasional Paper.

[135]The Evolution of the Desk (1980–2014). An initiative borne out of the Harvard Innovation Laboratory. The goal is to illustrate the impact that technology has had on our lives over the last 35 years. A cluttered desk,

complete with a rolodex, a file cabinet, and a fax machine, transforms into a much cleaner, simpler surface consisting of only a laptop and a mobile phone. Retrieved from https://www.youtube.com/watch?v=Z6PzTUDfxc0. Accessed on April 2017.

[136]http://www.zmescience.com/research/technology/smartphone-power-compared-to-apollo-432/

[137]Schwab, K. (2016 January 14). The Fourth Industrial Revolution: what it means, how to respond, WEF. Retrieved from https://www.weforum.org/agenda/2016/01/the-fourth-industrial-revolution-what-it-means-and-how-to-respond/. Accessed on April 2017.

[138]Unwin, J. (2016 November 24). Where next for civil society? Julia Unwin's inaugural lecture for the Wales Council for Voluntary Action (WCVA) given at their AGM. Retrieved from https://www.jrf.org.uk/where-next-civil-society. Accessed on April 2017.

[139]https://www.2degreesnetwork.com/services/collaboration-programs/

[140]Adler, R., Mehta, R., The National Alliance for Caregiving. (2014). Catalyzing technology to support family caregiving. Retrieved from http://www.caregiving.org/wp-content/uploads/2010/01/Catalyzing-Technology-to-Support-Family-Caregiving_FINAL.pdf. Accessed April 2017.

[141]Quoted in the "A Brave New World?" Accenture/BitC, November 2016.

[142]Claire, Z. (2016 March 22). This Non-profit Wants To Put Stay-At-Home Moms Back to Work, Fortune. Retrieved from http://fortune.com/2016/03/22/path-for-ward-returnship/ and Claire, Z. (2016 August 23). These six Tech Companies Are Recruiting Moms Who Left the Workplace. Fortune. Retrieved from http://fortune.com/2016/08/23/tech-jobs-mom-women-return-workplace/?xid=soc_socialflow_facebook_FORTUNE. Accessed on April 2017.

[143]Carers UK, & Employers for Carers. (2015). Caring and isolation in the Workplace: Impact report and recommendations. Retrieved from https://www.carersuk.org/for-professionals/policy/policy-library/caring-and-isolation-in-the-workplace. Accessed on April 2017.

[144]Triantafillou, J., et al. (2010). Informal care in the long-term care system: European Overview Paper, Athens/Vienna: Interlinks.

[145]Collinson, P. (2016). Self-employed set up co-operatives to share costs and services. *The Guardian*. 16 April. Retrieved from https://www.theguardian.com/money/2016/apr/16/self-employed-co-operatives-share-costs-srvices

[146]http://womensenews.org/2016/07/clinton-offers-quiet-policy-lure-to-millions-of-unpaid-caregivers/

[147]When WORK and CAREGIVING Collide: How Employers Can Support Their Employees Who Are Caregivers.

[148]Supporting Working Carers: The Benefits to Families, Business and the Economy 2013.

[149]Supporting Working Carers: The Benefits to Families, Business and the Economy 2013.

[150]Eurofound 2011 and author email exchange with Mezzo, July 2016.

[151]https://www.employersforcarers.org/about-us/efc-umbrella-membership

[152]Tearle, S. (2016 May 11). West Sussex County Council speaking at State of Caring Conference, London.

[153]Grayson, D., Nelson, J. Corporate Responsibility Coalitions: The Past, Present and Future of Alliances for Sustainable Capitalism Sheffield: Greenleaf Publishing; 2013.

[154]http://www.carersaustralia.com.au/international-conference/

[155]http://www.corporateknights.com/reports/global-100/

[156]ReACT represents nearly 1 million employees through its membership of more than 40 companies and non-profit organizations. ReACT seeks to create a supportive business environment where the challenges faced by caregivers juggling the demands of both work and caregiving for an adult with a chronic age-related disease are understood and recognised by employers so that employees can better meet their personal and professional responsibilities. Retrieved from www.respectcaregivers.org

[157]http://societyoflaterlifeadvisers.co.uk/ and conversation with SOLLA co-founder Brian Fisher, Aviva, Bristol, November 25 2016.

[158]'Collaborative Commitments' - A think-piece by Professor David Grayson, Doughty Centre for Corporate Responsibility, Cranfield School of Management, Prime Minister's Council on Social Action (2008).

[159]http://www.ndis.gov.au/

[160]The Economist, Pride & Prejudice, The global elite at the World Economic Forum will be getting in touch with its LGBT side, at last, January 2017.

[161]E-mail exchange with author January 2017.

[162]Martin, R., & Osberg, S. *Getting beyond better: How social entrepreneurship works.* New York, NY: Harvard Business Review Press; 2015.

[163]See for example Cannon, F. (2017). The Agility Mindset: How reframing flexible working delivers competitive advantage. Palgrave Macmillan 2017 and The Agile Future Forum. Retrieved from http://www.agilefutureforum.co.uk/. Accessed on April 15 2017.

# BIBLIOGRAPHY

Adler, R., & Mehta, R. (2014). *Catalyzing technology to support family caregiving*. The National Alliance for Caregiving.

Age UK & Carers UK. (2016). *Walking the tightrope: The challenges of combining work and care in later life*.

Buckner, L., & Yeandle, S. (2015). *Valuing Carers 2015: The rising value of carers support*. Carers UK.

Business in the Community. (2015). *Missing million*.

Carers Australia circa 2013: *Report No.1 — Combining work and care: The benefits to carers and the economy*; *Report No.2 — Combining work and care: The business case for carer-friendly workplaces*.

Carers Australia. (2015). *The economic value of informal care in Australia in 2015*.

Carers Canada. (2015). Work & Care a Balancing Act.

CIPD. (2016). *Creating longer, more fulfilling working lives: Employer practice in 5 European countries*. Policy Report and Policy Briefing.

Employers for Carers (2010). *The business case for supporting carers in and into work*. Employers for Carers and Carers UK, November. (A summary of this paper

was published in the Coalition Government's recent
'refresh' of the National Carers Strategy: Recognised,
valued and supported: next steps for the Carers Strategy
(November 2010) as Annex B: The evidence for supporting carers in work. The paper covers the demographic
drivers, the business case for employers, society and the
wider economy and includes employer case studies.)

Employers for Carers. (2011a). *Carers and employment:
Making a difference, realising potential.* Carers UK,
Employers for Carers and ADASS (Association of
Directors of Social Services), July. (With staff retention
and resilience a key challenge for employers large and
small, this practical guide shows how local authorities,
employers and other local stakeholders can have a real
impact on helping to retain and recruit carers into the
workforce. The guide (full and summary versions available) includes key recommendations, key drivers, including the business benefits of supporting carers, key tips
and practice examples.)

Employers for Carers. (2011b). *Caring at a distance:
Bridging the gap.* Carers UK, Employers for Carers and
Nomura, June. (This research examines the impacts on
employers and employees of managing caring at a distance. With our ageing population and workforce – and
increasing mobility through employment – managing
caring at a distance is moving centre stage as a business
issue. The research is based on a survey of around 1000
employees who have caring responsibilities at a distance,
along with 50 major employers. The pressure on the
"sandwich generation" emerges loud and clear – people,
often women, who are combining care for an older

relative with a range of other responsibilities including looking after their own children. Most respondents (60%) were in this age group – age 40 to 54 and reported the cumulative pressures of caring, not just the physical component but the mental aspect associated with stress, anxiety and tiredness.)

Employers for Carers. (2011c). *Conditions for employment for carers*. Employers for Carers and Carers UK, April. (This short position paper looks at the conditions for employment that EfC Leadership Group members want to see in order to support carers in and into the workplace. The paper covers key principles for employers, for services and for the development of the care market.)

Employers for Carers. (2012). *Sandwich caring*. (Today more and more parents are combining looking after young children with caring for older or disabled loved ones. This is sometimes called 'sandwich caring' or 'dual caring' and those who fall under this category are usually referred to as 'the sandwich generation'. But this dual role can sometimes come at a cost and carers may suffer from ill health, face difficulties to access or stay in the labour market or experience financial hardship. This Carers UK/Employers for Carers report looks at a specific category of sandwich carers, namely those 'who combine looking after a dependent child under the age of 18 with caring for an adult'. Despite rising awareness of this 'sandwich generation' it is difficult to get a clear understanding of the extent of the caring roles of the sandwich generation. Carers UK and Employers for Carers conducted this research as an attempt to better

understand the extra pressure these dual caring responsibilities have on modern families and their implications
for policy, public services, employers and the labour
market.)

Employers for Carers. (2013). *Supporting working carers:
The benefits families, business and the economy.* (The
Employers for Carers, Carers UK and HM Government
Task and Finish Group was set up in 2012 to explore
ways in which carers – people looking after a family
member or friend who is sick, ill or disabled – can be
supported to combine work and care. The final report
Supporting Working Carers sets out the findings and
recommendations for Government and employers. The
Task and Finish Group's work also included an
Employer Business Benefits Survey in which over 220
employers participated.)

Employers for Carers. (2014). *Supporting employees
who are caring for someone with dementia.* (With our
ageing population and workforce, dementia is becoming
an increasingly significant issue in the workplace, with
more and more people combining work with caring for
a loved one. In recognition of this, an employer and
employee survey was conducted between October 2013
and January 2014 to discover the impact of working
while also caring for someone with dementia. This
report sets out the key findings and emerging issues
from these surveys. It concludes by making 10 recommendations for employers, health and social care services and government to take to facilitate better support
for employees who are caring for loved ones with
dementia.)

Employers for Carers. (2015). *Caring and isolation in the workplace: Impact report and recommendations.* (With increased longevity and later retirement ages an increasing number of people in the UK are combining work and caring for older, ill or disabled relatives and friends. However, while one in nine people in any workplace will be supporting a loved one in this way, caring still remains a relatively hidden issue in the workplace, with many carers feeling lonely or isolated even when they may be part of a busy team or family unit. This survey of working carers highlights the isolation felt by thousands of carers in the workplace, with 38% indicating that they were not comfortable talking about their caring responsibilities at work. One in six working carers (16%) said that they felt isolated because they felt like they were the only person in this situation and over four in ten (43%) reported that their colleagues and managers did not understand the impact of these caring responsibilities. The research sets out how working carers can best be supported to minimise such isolation including through early advice, information and support and recommends practical ways in which employers and other parties can help.)

ETUC, Who Cares? (2011). *Experiences and possibilities to reconcile work and care responsibilities for dependent family members.*

Eurofound, European Foundation for the Improvement of Living and Working Conditions. (2011). *Company initiatives for workers with care responsibilities for disabled children or adults.*

Eurofound. (2015). *Working and caring: Reconciliation measures in times of demographic change*. Luxembourg: Publications Office of the European Union.

Government of Canada. (2015). *When work and caregiving collide: How employers can support their employees who are caregivers*. Report from the Employer Panel for Caregivers.

Goyer, A. (2015). *Juggling life, work, and caregiving*. AARP.

Kroger, T., & Yeandle, S. (2014). *Combining paid work and family care: Policies and experiences in international perspective*. Policy Press.

Minett, C., & Minett, R. (2011). *Action for ageing*. Vicheko Limited.

NAC & ReACT. (2012). *Best practices in workplace eldercare*.

Slaughter, A. M. (2015). *Unfinished business: Women men work family*.

# ACKNOWLEDGEMENTS

I argued at the outset that 'caring for working carers is like the missing jigsaw piece for several critical organisational strategies'. Writing a book often feels to me like completing a jigsaw puzzle too. Numerous friends and colleagues have helped me to put the jigsaw pieces of *Take Care* together. They include: Helena Herklots, Emily Holzhausen, Katherine Wilson, Madeleine Starr, Sue McLintock at Carers UK who have responded positively and creatively to my myriad queries and requests for information; and patiently explained why parts of the jigsaw puzzle are shaped as they are. Katherine in particular has been indefatigable in tracking down contacts and data. Ian Peters, honorary treasurer of Carers UK and chairman of Employers for Carers has challenged me to go deeper into the practicalities of caring for working carers and patiently responded to my suggestions about EfC. My Doughty Centre for Corporate Responsibility colleague Melody McLaren with whom I have periodically researched and written collaboratively for more than a quarter century, brought her own experience as a free-lance worker juggling work and caring for her husband, adding crucial extra pieces to the jigsaw – especially ideas about how freelancers can juggle working and caring. Thanks too to Lynne Lewis who meticulously typed up sections of the manuscript.

I am enormously grateful to everyone who agreed to be interviewed for Take Care; often subsequently searching out additional information and materials for me; and then securing organisational clearance for how I wrote up their stories and insights – often at extremely short notice. In particular, Caroline Waters who helped me find some of my first jigsaw pieces. My cousin Sue Briggs and my good friend Lainy Rodger helped me to see where some bits of the jigsaw puzzle fitted in better elsewhere than where I had put them initially. My partner in several books and many adventures, Adrian Hodges showed me clever ways of finding missing jigsaw pieces and how they might fit together. Colleagues in several of our Carers UK international sister organisations including Ara Cresswell (Carers Australia), Rachel Ledany (Caregivers Israel) and Rick Greene (National Alliance of Caregivers-USA) provided valuable insights and helpfully clarified that I was actually building a bigger, international jigsaw than the UK one I had actually started. Amanda Feldman and Amy Fetzer (Volans) introduced me to doctoral student Kaz Kobayashi who is researching Sustainable Human Capital and helped me to understand the work and care context in Japan. Michael Solomon of Responsible 100 helped me find more examples of how small businesses address the issue of work and care. It is always good to get an entirely fresh pair of eyes on any project and shortly before I handed over the manuscript, my friend Richard Hamilton generously 'volunteered' to read the almost completed text and made important suggestions for additional text.

Particular thanks to John Stuart and subsequently Pete Baker and Kerry Laundon and their Production team colleagues at Emerald Publishing who made sure that the jigsaw puzzle more or less matches the picture on the box; and all the packaging etc., is safe and sound and arrived safely.

A lifetime of thanks and love to my mum Patricia Grayson (1922–2015) who inspired me to go and find jigsaws and who right up until the end of her life, was encouraging me to lead the life I wanted to live and not the one that others wanted me to do.

A final thanks to my 'bro' Pawel Zabielski, who was there for me – especially during my mum's final months – and who can generally be relied upon to tell me when it is time to take a break from puzzles – jigsaws or otherwise. Thanks one and all.

# ABOUT THE AUTHOR

**David Grayson** is Professor of Corporate Responsibility at Cranfield University School of Management. He joined the world of management education in 2007 after a 30-year career as a social entrepreneur and campaigner for responsible business and diversity. This included founding Project North East (now PNE Group) — an innovative economic development social enterprise that has worked in nearly 60 countries), and serving as a Managing Director of the responsible business network Business in the Community. He has been a Visiting Senior Fellow at the CSR Initiative of Harvard's Kennedy School of Government and a Visiting Fellow at several UK and American business schools. David has chaired or served on various charity, social enterprise and public sector boards, including the National Co-operative Development Agency, The Prince of Wales' Innovation Trust, the Strategic Rail Authority, Housing21 and the National Disability Council. He currently chairs Carers UK. During his career, he has done work with numerous multinationals as well as for the OECD, EU and World Bank. He sits on the Corporate Responsibility stakeholder advisory groups for Camelot and for Lloyds Bank; is part of the Circle of Advisers for Business Fights Poverty and for the Asian Institute of Management's

Ramon V. del Rosario, Sr. Center for Corporate Social Responsibility. He is part of the faculty of The Forward Institute. He was awarded an OBE for services to industry in 1994 and a CBE for services to disability in 1999. David has written several books on responsible business, sustainability and social intrapreneurism. *The Guardian* has named David as one of 10 top global tweeters on sustainable leadership alongside Al Gore, Tim Cook (CEO of Apple), Sheryl Sandberg (COO of Facebook) and Kumi Naidoo (the head of Greenpeace International). @DavidGrayson_

# INDEX